The Art of Less Doing

THE
ART
OF
LESS
DOING

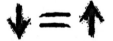

One Entrepreneur's Formula
for a Beautiful Life

ARI MEISEL

THE ART OF LESS DOING

One Entrepreneur's Formula

for a Beautiful Life

ISBN   978-1-61961-442-0   *Paperback*

        978-1-61961-443-7   *Ebook*

For my daughter Chloe, the
final piece of the puzzle.

CONTENTS

. . .

INTRODUCTION

. . .

THE WAKE-UP CALL

Ten years ago, I was diagnosed with Crohn's disease, a chronic, extremely painful inflammation of the digestive tract. At the time, I was living a very unhealthy and stressful lifestyle, working fourteen-hour days and basically being a hard-charging workaholic. In short, I was behaving like the average American twenty-something male.

The pain became so bad at one point that my girlfriend (now my wife) and I went to the hospital to have it checked out. After he ran a few tests, the doctor left the diagnosis on my voice mail, which was an additional kick in my already wounded gut. I had to Google Crohn's disease, which is the worst way to get medical information. The online descriptions of the disease were terrifying. (Just some of the buzzwords swimming around were colon cancer, surgery, pain, death.)

A second opinion confirmed the diagnosis, but at least I was working with a doctor with a modicum of bedside manner. With Crohn's, or any autoimmune disease, there are levels of intensity to the drug regime. I started with the mildest, which had the least side effects, but was also not terribly effective. Finally, we landed on something that worked.

There are several theories as to what causes the disease. There is a strong genetic predisposition. Two thirds of people afflicted are Ashkenazi Jews, and I'm half Ashkenazi, half Sephardi. It typically occurs in people under the age of thirty: I was under twenty-five at the time of diagnosis. Another contributing factor is severe gut dysbiosis, which is when antibiotics, stress, processed foods, smoking, and things of that nature compromise your gut bacteria. The immune system starts attacking healthy intestinal tissue, which leads to a whole host of other problems. The fix is to protect gut bacteria through probiotics, eating good fats, reducing stress, and sleeping better. Most of it comes down to diet and stress management, also significant contributing factors to the disease.

One of the problems with Western medicine is that we

treat the symptoms and not the cause, which was what I did initially. I just wanted relief, and the prescriptions helped. At first, I didn't even think about changing my lifestyle or my habits. Every few months, I would get sick again and take the pills. This went on for a few years until one particular incident led to an epiphany. After a night of overeating and drinking, my system revolted against me. I wound up back in the hospital, racked with pain, with a 105° temperature for days.

Something had to give. It became clear to me that I could no longer just be a passenger on my own medical journey. I had to get in the driver's seat and take control. I was at war with my body, and I needed to get my battle gear on.

My path to real recovery started with data. I had been undergoing extensive blood testing every five weeks, so I had a lot of diagnostic information about my blood. I created spreadsheets and crunched numbers, and even though I didn't necessarily unearth any revealing information, I had a deeper sense of control. I felt like I was finally beginning to take an active role in my condition, which was the little push I needed to advance forward.

Diet and fitness were the next frontier. I dove into a new routine directly opposite of everything I had been doing before. I ditched meat and became a vegetarian for six months and later a pescatarian for close to three years. I've always enjoyed working out, but in my early twenties, I was pumping iron and taking systemic steroids for the Crohn's. I was ripped, but in an inflamed, angry man kind of way, and I was destroying my body. Instead, I found the most intense workout program I've ever seen, Insanity, and committed myself to it like a religion. Sure, it took me close to three weeks to finish a single workout, but after sixty days I lost twenty-two pounds!

My personal approach in those days was a bit extreme, but that's the way I am by nature, and it's what my body needed. Aside from losing weight and feeling better, I became addicted to the increased sense of control I had over my body. I was no longer letting something bad "just happen" to me. The sense of accomplishment from making better decisions was immediate.

Around the same time that I was going through my physical transformation, I started blogging about productivity. I wanted to devise a system to counter chronic stress and fatigue and to help people to feel better, to place a higher value on their time, and, ultimately, to lead better lives. The fact that the illness limited my workday forced me to find new and innovative ways to accomplish more in less time. I hadn't yet devised my system of "Less Doing, More Living," but it was percolating through the blog posts. I knew the best way to test the validity of the concepts was to teach a class, which I did. Through student feedback and personal trial and error, the program crystallized.

A FRAMEWORK FOR LIFE

What would you do if you only worked for one hour per day? Would you crumble or would you thrive? Just close your eyes for a minute and imagine a new reality for yourself. One in which you have plenty of time to do the things you really want to do with the people you care about. This new reality is completely within reach! It simply involves figuring out how to work efficiently and in much smaller amounts of time so you can put your energy elsewhere. It requires questioning what is possible on a high level and then breaking it down.

Everyone has different needs and pressures, so the end result will vary according to the individual. However, the basic tenants are applicable to everyone. We could all use a little more time in our day, and the method of finding it is universal. Through a philosophy anchored in the concept of "less," virtually anyone can learn to streamline their workload and become more efficient in their day-to-day activities. By doing less, you will experience profound transformation and be able to take back your life across all spectrums: at work, at home, and in your mind.

The productivity framework I lay out in this book focuses on three concepts: optimize, automate, and outsource. Each of the three components is widely applicable and serves in different and important ways to simplify activities that can lead to damaging chronic stress. My methodology will ask you to think about and approach everyday tasks in a whole new way.

The first step in designing a work-life balance that works for you is to identify how you spend your time. Once you have a better understanding of how you're approaching everyday activities and how long they take, you'll start to see that there are several things you can say no to or let go of entirely. Data collection, self-tracking, and analysis are key elements of transformation.

If you're working in a corporate environment with strict hours, you can apply the principles in this book to certain areas of your professional life and widely across your personal life. The last thing anyone wants or needs is to leave a hectic and stressful day at the office and find the same environment at home. There are systems and solutions to make your home life run like a well-oiled machine. Similarly, you can apply these principles to your health, which is where it all began for me. Cognitive therapy, sleep hacking, supplementation, and a variety of other methods can greatly enhance your biological performance. You can improve your personal finances by adding additional income streams through very little effort. The point is these strategies are designed specifically for people who feel they do not have flexibility or choices. The truth is everyone does, and I'll show you how to find and use both.

The purpose of this book is to share a systematic method to optimize, automate, and outsource the bulk of the tasks that fill up our personal and professional lives. The "Less Doing, More Living" Method is guaranteed to free up precious time and energy to allow you to pursue more meaningful endeavors that lead to personal joy and fulfillment. Through the process, you'll be able to enjoy your life (and preserve your sanity) at work and at home. Start living the life you want to live and spend your time doing the things you care about. Focus on what matters. Your life is calling.

PART I

...

OPTIMIZE

THE FIRST STEP IN THE JOURNEY TOWARD "LESS" is optimization. This means breaking down any challenge you face to its bare minimum, streamlining it, and eliminating anything that's not completely necessary. Optimizing asks you to stop and examine exactly what you are doing and how. What is the specific task at hand and how can you simplify it even further? This question leads to devising systems for efficiency. If you are extremely diligent in your approach, it is feasible to create a scenario in which you are working a maximum of one to two hours per day, or one to two days a week. It's a matter of finding what works for you and your life.

Tim Ferriss introduced the idea of the minimal effect dosage in his *4-Hour Body* book. His theory is that we should focus on the smallest action that will produce a desired outcome, and anything beyond that is wasteful. We should not try to do the most possible; we should try to do the least necessary. The concept has a negative connotation for some people, because they see the approach as an inadequate effort, but in fact, the opposite is true. If you're overdoing something or you're misallocating resources, you're doing it inefficiently. Just because you are doing more, does not mean it is better. When you start to look at an activity from this perspective, there is a mind shift. Less is more, and quality is king.

The 4-Hour Workweek, Ferriss's first book, was a number-one *New York Times* best seller for seven years because the concept of living more and working less resonates in an enormous way with people. Tim, by the way, has never worked as little as four hours in a week. The man is a serial entrepreneur and angel investor, and he loves what he does. He has, however, mastered the art of redesigning life to get what he wants out of it. By optimizing your time and understanding how you spend it, you too can redesign the way you work and have the life you want.

One

KNOW THYSELF

* * *

THE MULTITASKING MYTH

As a productivity consultant, I can say with confidence that most people do not self-identify as unproductive. In fact, highly functioning people tend to think they could always do more. On the flip side, there are also people who delude themselves into thinking that they are highly functioning multitaskers, when in fact they spread themselves so thin, nothing ever really gets done and certainly not done very well. These misconceptions regarding personal productivity boil down to a complete lack of self-awareness.

Humans have not evolved biologically as quickly as they have technologically. It's unrealistic to think we should be neurologically able to manage the constant barrage of information and never-ending stimuli that comes at us in a given day. Our brains can't process all of the stuff coming in, so they shut down in response.

For example, think about your e-mail inbox. Does the mere thought of it cause you a feeling of panic or a sense of dread? If you're like most people, your blood pressure has already shot up a few notches, you've stopped reading this book, and you're checking your e-mail. I've worked with people who have literally thousands of unopened e-mails taunting them on any regular day. It's so overwhelming; they don't even want to look at their inbox.

E-mail has become the ultimate paradigm shift. When used properly, it is one of the greatest productivity tools ever invented. There's no other communication resource available that is completely free, enables you to be in touch with people around the globe, share images and documents, and file it all. And yet, look at how the average businessperson views e-mail! It's one of many examples of things people deem to be difficult or impossible, until you show them the solution, and then anyone can do it.

---

https://en.wikipedia.org/wiki/Egg_of_Columbus

Most of the incredible communication tools we have at our disposal—cell phones, instant messaging, social media platforms, for example—have become leashes and obligations, rather than the productivity tools they are intended to be. The tools lead to feeling overwhelmed, but most people don't know what is causing them to feel that way. And around and around the circle goes. People get caught up in the cycle, and it's hard for them to recognize when they are actually producing good work. The overall feeling is one of dissatisfaction, which causes an inability to take advantage of the resources that could make their lives easier. People have lost touch with what technology can do for them and instead have developed a very unhealthy relationship with it. If you have good habits, technology can make them better. If you have bad habits, it will intensify those habits.

Biologically, humans are designed to focus on one thing at a time. Therefore, multitasking is not an activity the human brain is capable of handling. The neurological term for multitasking is "context switching." When we attempt to multitask, we switch back and forth between tasks so quickly that we physically exhaust our brains.

People have tried to "game the system" by combining low-focus activities with high-focus activities to train the brain to be better at context switching. Interestingly, women are marginally (2–3 percent) better at context switching than men, but generally speaking, switching back and forth between tasks is completely mentally exhausting. Most people cannot focus on a single task for longer than five minutes without getting distracted.

In exercise, the multitasking phenomenon is called the central governor theory. It proposes that the brain is self-regulating and will literally shut down before the body can over exert. The theory supports why running on a treadmill tends to be more exhausting than running outside. A treadmill has more stimuli to keep track of, including calories burned, time, heart rate, incline, and a variety of other information blinking and beeping at you. It's a lot to take in when you're trying to blow off some steam!

THE 80/20 RULE

The 80/20 Rule, also known as the Pareto Principle, promotes the concept of identifying the things in your life that give you the most bang for your buck. Pareto was an Italian economist and an avid gardener. He was surveying his plants one day and noticed that 20 percent of his pea plants produced 80 percent of the peas. The concept enchanted him, and so he and scratched a little further to discover a similar phenomenon occurred within the economy: 80 percent of the land was owned by 20 percent of the population. He surveyed other countries as well and found the same ratio applied. The overall observation is that most things in life are not distributed evenly.

What are the things that require the least amount of effort but have the greatest return on investment? In business, this rule means that 20 percent of your clients are responsible for 80 percent of your income. The other 80 percent of your clients are essentially gobbling up your time and energy with no return. Pareto (and Tim Ferriss) would argue that you should cease paying attention to that 80 percent and concentrate solely on the 20 percent that is making you money.

For example, say you have five clients who are paying you $10,000/month. They're loyal and they'll be with you well into the future. Additionally, you have one hundred clients with whom you work with sporadically. They spend about $50/month and they always complain. Those low-paying clients suck up a lot of energy and time, and they're simply not worth the limited income. Focus on the lucrative few.

If you apply this principle to your e-mail inbox, you could easily eliminate close to 60–75 percent of the volume. Set a filter to file every e-mail that has the word "unsubscribe" in it to an optional folder. That way, all of those e-mails will immediately bypass your inbox, thereby greatly reducing the feeling of being overwhelm. The lower number of unopened e-mails taunting you will allow you to focus on the messages that are of the highest importance.

This practice differs from using SaneBox or an app that creates folders, because the filter creates two different buckets in which you operate differently. Your inbox is a place for work, for productivity, and for getting things done. The optional folder is the opposite; it holds e-mails that do not require your immediate attention. The beauty of this system is that, knowing all of the e-mails in your optional folder are optional, you can fly through them much faster when you're ready to give them your attention.

The 80/20 Rule fits into my concept of Less Doing, More Living because I believe that 20 percent of your effort and resources should be devoted to work, while the other 80 percent should be allocated toward rest, relaxation, and personal development. In that vein, I spend 80 percent of my time with my family, exercising, eating, reading, sleeping, or learning. Because I've made the choice to spend my time this way, I'm forced to figure out ways to be ultraproductive when I am working.

I've optimized all of the activities in my home and work life so that I am spending the maximum amount of my energy doing what gives me the highest reward in the moment. I run my whole business from my phone, which means I am 100 percent mobile. I've reorganized my time so I can focus on my wife and kids, because family is what matters the most to me.

My work schedule often revolves around my kids' nap and school schedules. When my twin boys are napping, I'll crank out an hour of work. After my wife and I have dinner together and put the kids to bed, I'll sit down for another hour and half of work. I've identified pockets of time in the day when I can focus uninterrupted and am able to be the most productive. I would never be able to work this way if I didn't have systems that allow me to work in the most time-efficient and concentrated manner. Honestly, I would love to work forty hours a week because I love what I do with Less Doing, but I'm a huge believer in setting restrictions that force us to be more effective.

Imagine if you had to give up e-mail. Do you think it's impossible? Look at John Paul DeJoria, the founder of Paul Mitchell hair products and the premium tequila brand, Patrón, among other ventures. He's worth four billion dollars and the man has never had an e-mail address or owned a computer. It's not impossible. You just have to "figure it out." Mitchell says he would be so inundated by the technology that he would never get any work done!

DeJoria does all of his business in person or on the phone, and his philosophy is to "pay attention to the vital few and ignore the trivial many." Words to live by!

AWARENESS THROUGH TRACKING

The best way to start optimizing your time, energy, and resources is to start tracking things at work and at home. You need to be able to identify metrics and patterns before you can start to adjust or eliminate activities or behaviors. Start by tracking what you're working on, how long it takes, how many things you are doing at once, how much money you spend on food, how many times you ate at your desk, and any other habitual activities or behaviors that you're interested in changing or getting rid of. Once you begin to track and attach numbers to your day-to-day routine, not only are you affording yourself the opportunity to improve, but psychologically you will have an increased sense of control in an otherwise overwhelming environment.

The data collection time frame will vary according to the individual and the activity being tracked. Recently, I was working with a client who wanted me to help him with his nutrition. Initially, we thought we'd need a month, or at least a week, of data, but after just two days of looking at his food log, the problem revealed itself. He was texting photos of his meals and caloric intake at the end of each day, and I noticed a Starbucks Frappuccino bottle in the background of one of his pictures. There are 32 grams of sugar in just one of those tiny bottles, and he was drinking those things all day. He hadn't even realized how much sugar he was taking in, so in his case, just two days was long enough to start making changes. One small adjustment can have a massive impact. In this case, it was a single beverage.

Let's look at personal finance. Money is something that a lot of people would like to have better control over. There never seems to be enough to fill all of the buckets that need filling. The app, Mint, is a fantastic way to track where you are spending all of those precious dollars. It syncs with your bank account, and in just a week's time, you'll have enough data to analyze your spending behaviors. You may not even be aware that you're eating out four nights a week or spending $300/week on groceries. The morning double half-caf cappuccino probably adds up to much more than you think. If you're someone who has a hard time finding $1,000 for your savings account, take a close look at your daily spending habits to determine what you can minimize or eliminate altogether.

How you spend your time is also valuable information. Parkinson's Law says, "Work expands to fill the time allotted to complete it." Many people need a sense of urgency to get things done. If you're a procrastinator, you'll use up all of the time you have allotted for a project and then likely finish it at the eleventh hour. This behavior is largely based on personality, but generally speaking, if you have a task to do and a half an hour to do it, you will probably get it done. If you have an hour to do the same task, you'll probably take the whole hour to do it. I'm guilty of this myself, which is one of the reasons I live and die by my Google calendar. I put every activity, meeting, and phone call in my calendar to set a parameter for myself.

Once you start tracking how you spend your time, you'll find that you're wasting hours on unproductive behaviors. Many times, wasted time doesn't even relate to stress; it's simply due to the fact that you have time to waste. Be aware that just because you're tracking something, it doesn't necessarily mean that you will find an immediate correlation. For example, tracking weight and losing weight do not go hand in hand, unfortunately.

Sleep is another often-overlooked area that is easy to track. The results generally have a large impact. You don't need to assess the reasons why you have a bad sleep necessarily; all you need to track is whether you had a good sleep or a bad sleep. College students are notoriously the most sleep-deprived demographic.

Brown University conducted a famous sleep research study in 2001. The twist was they told the students who had slept poorly that they had in fact slept very well and vice versa. Then, the students completed a series of cognitive tests. Their performance was based directly on how they were told they had slept. This is not the placebo effect, but the power of suggestion. Even those who had slept poorly trusted the data over how they actually felt, which just goes to show the power of information and the control it has over performance. Naïve realism is a philosophy rooted in the theory of perception. It claims that the senses provide us with direct awareness of the external world, and we should take objects at face value.

As human beings, we tend to be very sure of ourselves and have strong opinions, but we can also be very weak when it comes to defending those opinions. We have a tendency to convince ourselves that however we go about a certain task is exactly the correct way of going about it. For example, if I am driving down the road at seventy-five miles per hour, and someone passes me going eighty, I'll think that guy is a lunatic. And if I'm stuck behind someone else who is driving seventy, I'll honk my horn at him and think he is the world's worst slowpoke.

Basically, we tend to think that whatever we're doing is the baseline for appropriate action, and we form very strong opinions about others' behaviors. In the driving example, I think, "That guy going eighty is a complete nut! He's breaking the law! Even though, technically, I also was breaking the law, that other guy was breaking the law more. And that slowpoke back there! Has he never heard you pass on the left and travel in the right lane? Where did these people learn to drive?" Being aware of your behaviors and attitudes, so that you can employ some sort of helping mechanism to adjust, is the solution.

The first step of optimizing is identification. If you are averse to technology, you can simply start to track behaviors and time in a journal or a notebook. Start with any area of your life that you want to improve and start small. If you want to lose weight, track what foods you are eating. If you feel strapped for time, track how you're spending it. You can't optimize a behavior or an activity until you first identify it and then understand your current patterns.

Tracking time and behaviors is also a fantastic way to regain a sense of control over your life. Knowledge is power and that applies to being overwhelmed as well. When you can identify the areas in your day or life that are causing your stress, gobbling up your time, or devouring your resources, you can develop action steps toward change. For most people, it adds a quantitative element to an otherwise qualitative measurement.

Three Steps to Less

1. Collect data by tracking your time, energy, and resources to identify patterns.

2. Focus on one thing at a time. Eliminate multitasking and other unproductive behaviors.

3. Implement the Pareto Principle (the 80/20 Rule). Focus on the things in your life that give you the highest return on investment.

Two

THE EXTERNAL
BRAIN

· · ·

HUMANS HAVE A VERY LIMITED WORKING MEMORY.
One of the reasons phone numbers are seven digits—ten
with the area code—is because we don't have the capacity
to remember longer numbers. Similarly, we have a hard
time holding on to the thoughts or ideas that we don't
have time to deal with in the moment. If we don't record
them somewhere (and fast), *poof*, they've gone to the
great idea boneyard. What system do you have in place
to record your ideas so you don't lose them?

The concept behind the external brain comes from the
external hard drive on a computer. Like your laptop, your
brain can only hold and process so much information at

one time. We need a way to off-load ideas and knowledge, and we need a place to store them safely. Every tiny action needs a system for efficiency. In creating those systems, we increase the flow of more pressing ideas and information so that we can better handle them unencumbered.

At the heart of the information off-loading process is the simple act of note taking. Essentially, it comes down to a data dump in which key ideas are transferred from one system (your brain) to another (a notebook or an app). This approach helps you to get the things you want to learn more about, take advantage of, or develop out of your head and into a safe storage location. Then you can set reminders to yourself to take action on them at a later time. This process improves mental capacity and functionality, but it also allows you to design a system so that you have constant universal access to everything you know. Seth Godin, the marketing guru, likes to say that anything worth memorizing is worth looking up.

How many times have you had an amazing idea in the shower? Stanford University actually conducted a research study on the phenomenon of shower inspiration. Science has proven that people tend to think more creatively when they're in a warm and happy place. Plus, we are less emotionally inhibited when we are naked, which makes perfect sense. How many times has your amazing idea slipped right out of your mind the minute you turn off the faucet and stepped out of the shower? It's the most frustrating experience not only because you've lost the idea, but chances are it was a really good one!

We use Aquanotes at our house, which are basically waterproof post-it notes. Originally scuba divers used them, but anyone can stick them in their home shower to capture their best ideas and get it out of their heads. The brain is great at coming up with ideas, but it's not so great at holding on to them. Instead of fighting against our natural human tendencies, we must learn to adapt to them.

As mentioned previously, we have not evolved biologically as quickly as we have technologically. It's not reasonable on any level to expect to keep up. The spoken word is 150,000 years old, but the written word is only 30,000 years old. Even professional writers will tell you that it is very difficult to sit down and write. The reason for this is that writing is not ingrained in our DNA as deeply as storytelling through speech. Most people are pretty good at talking, but far fewer people are good at writing. Excel spreadsheets were only invented thirty years ago, which introduces a whole new challenge.

The human brain can only handle so much. We need to treat it like the precious resource it is and protect it. By overloading it with stimuli and never giving it a break through off-loading, we're asking too much of it. Embracing the concept of the external brain allows your actual internal brain to do its best work and come up with the most creative and inspired ideas.

One of my favorite tools to capture ideas is Evernote. It's extremely convenient because it works across all platforms. You can effectively off-load your ideas no matter what you are doing or where you are. The system allows you to capture anything: a written note, a photograph, an audio recording, a YouTube video, a blog post, a *New York Times* article. There are extensions for all your devices, so you can clip and save any information you want, whether you're on your laptop, tablet, or phone. But what's even better is once your Evernote starts to populate with clippings, it will show you related or connected notes. It intuitively organizes your ideas for you and makes them easier to access and develop, all within the app. The more information you put into it, the better it will function for you. At this point, I have close to 15,000 notes stored in Evernote. It magically connects the dots and draws correlations that the human brain cannot handle or possibly remember.

Brain activity is a lot like traffic on a highway. It needs to flow. For every minute of stoppage on the highway, it takes forty minutes for traffic to return to a normal flow. Similarly, every minute that you take away from a core activity, or spend distracted by something else, it takes about twenty-three minutes to get back into that flow state of productivity. Those distracted moments represent an enormous opportunity cost, and most people don't get back into the flow state until the next day. One distraction tends to lead to another and has a compounding effect.

Psychologists and behaviorists have been studying the brain for over a century. Bluma Zeigarnik was a Russian doctoral student in Berlin in the '20s. She hypothesized that a specific part of our brain processes open-ended information. As human beings, we have a natural tendency toward closure in that we like to finish things. Even the worst procrastinators like to complete their tasks. She also noted that once a task is complete, people tend to forget the details associated with it. Only when the task is interrupted or incomplete are people able to remember the details. She designed a series of experiments to test and better understand this phenomenon, which eventually became known as the Zeigarnik Effect.

Zeigarnik's theory became the basis of an important activity related to increased productivity. Francesco Cirillo developed his time management method, the Pomodoro Technique, in the '80s. The technique uses a timer to break work into fixed intervals, usually twenty-five minutes, separated by short (five-minute) breaks. The method is based on the idea that frequent breaks can improve mental agility. So fixed and focused activities are most effectively executed through timed interruptions. When the timer goes off, you can do anything you want for five minutes and then sit back down again and get into focused concentration. Your productivity is measured by the amount of work intervals you've completed, aptly referred to as Pomodoros.

WHY TO-DO LISTS ARE BAD

Using the Pomodoro Technique is different than crossing items off of your to-do list. With the interval approach, your focus is on productivity over tasks completed. Inevitably, several tasks will be completed during the Pomodoro intervals. The interruption, as we saw with the Zeigarnik Effect, makes it so you can work in a sprint and then take a very quick break. Your brain will have had an opportunity to rest in between work cycles, and it will work more efficiently because of the interruption. Research shows, metaphorically speaking, that our minds work better in sprints than they do in marathons.

The Zeigarnik Effect, at its heart, is the voice in our heads that pushes us to complete the uncompleted task. This feeds into one of the main problems with to-do lists. Most of the items on the list are not things that you can accomplish immediately, either because they are too big to do in a day, or you're waiting on someone else. Nevertheless, our brain scans the list, it sees a series of things that it cannot yet complete, and the Zeigarnik Effect kicks in. No matter how conscientious you've been about prioritizing your list, the brain looks for tasks that can be completed next, which creates cognitive dissonance. It puts the brakes on your productivity, which is the opposite of optimizing.

My personal disdain for to-do lists is a leftover from my days in LEED green construction. I had a company that did consultations in the green building industry, which is likely one of the most inefficient systems I have ever encountered. There are mountains of paperwork to contend with, and you're always waiting on something from someone else, which will stop a project dead in its tracks. I found myself with lists and lists of things I needed to do, but I had no control over any of them. It was insanely frustrating. I had to develop a different relationship with these lists or I was going to go crazy.

I started thinking about the question of "when" I could

do something instead of "what" was on the list. When could I get the permit? When could I review the engineer's plans? When did the city planning department need to have our paperwork? This transformed my to-do list into more of a hands-on exercise. I took the existing system and broke it into much smaller steps that were easier to manage and mapped it all out on the calendar.

I don't believe in priorities. To me, they are just a step above useless. I believe in finding the best time to do something. No matter how much of a burning priority the task may be, if you are not functioning in an optimal work zone, the work will suffer. For example, I know that I cannot do any creative work before 8:00 p.m. I have to be in the right frame of mind and the house needs to be quiet so I can focus. If the *Daily Beast* sends me an e-mail asking for an article, I defer it using an app called followup. cc, and don't even think about it until after eight when I can focus. If I attempted to write an article at 10:30 in the morning when I'm at the peak of my kid's activities, it would be a terrible, discombobulated mess.

When I was in high school, my brain was flooded with business ideas. I kept one of those black and white Mead marbled notebooks on me at all times. I jotted down the ideas as they came to me, an early incarnation of the external brain. By the time I graduated from college, I lost touch with the practice of writing everything down and the stream of ideas slowed. I worried that I was losing my creativity. The fact is that my brain was overloaded with so much everyday stuff; there was no room for flowing ideas. There is a limited amount of space in our brains for memories, for working on things, and for problem solving, and the more that you hold in your brain, the less you can use your brain to its fullest capabilities.

There needs to be an external factor that allows you to expand your mind in one way or another and learn new concepts. Maybe it's reading blogs or nonfiction books or maybe it's learning a new trade. You're not going to grow as a human being if you don't pursue areas of interest outside of your chosen profession.

For example, one of my coaching clients had an education company, and he was doing extremely well with it. But he's always been interested in boat building, so now he is taking a class in the subject. He's never done anything that involved working with his hands and physically building something from scratch, but he absolutely loves it. I'm convinced this experience will be one of the keys to unlocking what he wants to do next in his career.

Some of the best ideas I've ever had came to me when I took a welding class at the 3rd Ward in Brooklyn. The experience challenged my brain and my hands in new ways. It took me out of myself and put me in a situation I would likely never find myself in otherwise. These types of situations allow our minds to open up to new possibilities.

Increasing productivity is all about finding systems that work for you, not other people. Your active brain should contain only the bare minimum amount of information you need in a given moment. When you can off-load the bulk of the noise and the junk to an external hard drive, you give your brain the opportunity to focus on only the most essential items.

Three Steps to Less

1. Off-load ideas and knowledge for safe storage and to free up brain space.

2. Get rid of your to-do list.

3. Implement the Pomodoro Technique to maximize work efficiency. Work in sprints, not marathons.

Three

THE HOUR
OF POWER

. . .

FIND YOUR FLOW STATE

Every day, each one of us has roughly a ninety-minute period of peak productivity. This peak period is when you are able to produce your best work, but it is also the time frame within which you can most easily get into a work mode. You are more able to access the faculties of your mind, your body, and your nervous system. If you identify that time, respect it, and use it effectively to focus, you should be able to be two to one hundred times more effective than during any other time of the day. In this regard, knowing your peak time is extremely liberating. This also makes the question, "What would you do if you could only work one hour each day?" a reality.

The number one effect of flow state (peak performance, the sweet spot, being in the zone) is that time dilates. Seconds feel like hours, or hours feel like seconds. Everyone has a peak flow period and it's different for all of us. Personally, my peak time is between 10:00 a.m. and noon, and I make sure to schedule my day accordingly.

One of my clients told me that she woke up at 4:00 a.m. every morning with her mind racing. I suggested that that might be her peak time, and she should probably get up and experiment with it. It turned out to be an amazing window of productivity for her. She thought it was anxiety. Most people don't believe that an hour of power exists. If they do, they often don't know to identify it, let alone respect it.

Initially, the racing thoughts at four in the morning frustrated my client; she just wanted them to go away so she could get back to sleep. Only after she had a full grasp of the importance of identifying and utilizing her hour of power was she able to capitalize on its usefulness. Now, instead of wasting that precious time, she makes the most of it. Plus, the added benefit of her unique peak time is that no one else is awake in her house, and she can crank without distractions.

My company recently created an app called Less Doing Peak Time to help people identify their unique period of peak productivity. It's based on the central nervous system tap test, which has been around for decades. The tap test has been used to assess motor control in everyone from astronauts to Olympic athletes. The premise behind it is absurdly simple. Basically, someone taps their finger on their phone screen for ten seconds and the app counts the number of taps.

Research has proven that the tap test is an extremely good corollary to the health and recovery state of the nervous system. If you're a hard-charging athlete, and you tackle a really hard workout one day, the next day your tap test is going to be lower. I hypothesized that if you did the test a few times a day at different intervals, you would be able to identify the time of day (on average) that your nervous system is firing on all cylinders. It turned out to be true.

All of my clients are using the app, and we've discovered some very interesting things. One of my clients' peak time is at 5:00 p.m., which is highly unusual. That's the time of day when most people have completely depleted their mental capacity for the day. She blocks off an hour and a half of the day from 5:00 p.m. to 6:30 p.m. to focus on her most important tasks, and it's worked out beautifully for her.

If you respect your hour of power and make time for it by scheduling it, you are in essence respecting yourself and your capabilities. You're using your brain for what it should be used for, and you're maximizing its potential. This has a gratifying effect because you know you're getting things accomplished and doing them to the best of your ability.

I work with a lot of people who have standard nine to five, or even seven to seven corporate jobs. They're putting in the eight (plus) hours, but at the end of the day, they feel they haven't accomplished much. This is a very common feeling and one that most certainly leads to a sense of being overwhelmed. When people are able to respect and utilize their peak time, they can then feel a sense of freedom knowing they did the best that they could during their peak productivity time. The rest of the day is just gravy on top. Progress begets progress and is therefore intrinsically motivating. If you feel like you're moving in the right direction, you're going to keep heading that way.

ZONE OUT

Just as we all have an hour of power in our days, we also all have a brain-dead part of the day. David Allen, productivity expert and author of *Getting Things Done*, advocates having a "brain-dead" list of activities that you can accomplish when you've exhausted your mental capacity to function at a high level. To make the most of your time, you need to utilize even the downtime hours when you're feeling tired or sluggish. Zoning out, as opposed to being in the zone, has a direct relationship with mindful meditation, which is always a beneficial undertaking.

When you feel like zoning out, there are a number of activities that don't require your top-level focus such as preparing food, light housekeeping, or straightening up around the house. Even catching up with the news or checking social media can be relaxing and nontaxing.

Personally, I use my brain-dead hour to process over one thousand blog posts. I don't necessarily have to read each one in detail and prepare a report on the content. It's just a source of ideas for me for my own blog posts and podcasts. If something catches my eye, I'll clip it to Evernote for a deeper dive when I have more brainpower. I find comfort in knowing when my downtimes are. Because they are balanced with hours of power, I can more easily accept the fact that I am not on all the time—no one is—and see those brain-dead hours for what they are.

OPTIMIZING THE POWER HOUR

One of my clients is a psychology consultant. He's in the habit of creating short, five-minute, daily videos for his clients, and he films them at 11:00 p.m. every night. They're really excellent; each video focuses on a specific concept he wants to address that day. His clients love them and look forward to them. They are a big driver of business for him.

This same client came to me because he was frustrated. He was struggling to delegate within his company, and he simply did not have time during the day to train his staff on what they needed to know. He was growing irritated with his situation. We came up with the idea that he should simply make training videos for his staff in addition to the videos he was already making for his clients. It was a medium he was comfortable with, it's a personal way of conveying information, and he had already staked out a quiet part of the evening for filming.

We took the idea one step further and decided he should also make a third video of himself, for himself, and treat it like a video journal. He could off-load his top-of-mind thoughts of the day and have something tangible to refer back to. The extra videos have worked out for him in a big way. Now he uses that hour of power—from 11:00 p.m. to 12:00 pm—to create his three videos. His staff has access to valuable resources that enable them to do what they do better, which in turn enables him to do what he does better. It came down to accessing something that he was already doing and optimizing it within the hour that he was at his very best. It's important to recognize that when you are feeling blocked from conveying a message, you should look at the method of communication.

In my own schedule, I value the activities slotted in my peak time more highly than anything else. If the world is falling down around me, it would take an act of God for me to cancel my peak time appointments and activities. Canceling would cause me to feel very frustrated and resentful of whatever got in the way. If all else fails, and I am able to squeeze in an hour and half of productivity, I feel good, which is half the battle to begin with!

Optimizing is about throwing out all of the excess and stress of a standard workweek and crafting your own plan instead. Finding and respecting that hour of power is one of the key ways to be the designer of your day and to keep your sanity at the same time. Enjoy the sense of accomplishment that comes with discovering, using, and respecting your peak time. It's yours for the taking.

Three Steps to Less

1. Identify your hour of peak productivity with the Less Doing Peak Time app.

2. Respect and optimize your hour of power.

3. Utilize "downtime" by churning through low-focus tasks.

Four

SETTING LIMITS

· · ·

WITH A LITTLE ATTITUDE SHIFT AND SOME DISCI-
pline, it is possible to set limits on practically anything:
calorie intake, the amount of hours worked, your budget,
your digital and/or carbon footprint, and almost anything
under the sun. Setting limits is directly related to one's
mind-set.

SANCTIONED CLOCK WATCHING

Most of my clients would fall into the workaholic category.
They tend to stay at the office until all hours, to the detri-
ment of their family life and their personal health. One
of the first ways that I try to set limits on people who fall
into this category is to restrict the number of hours they
spend at the office. I suggest they leave everyday at 5:00
p.m., depending on the person and their work schedule.

This suggestion is usually greeted with a lot of hemming and hawing. The first few days of trying to limit the number of hours at the office are always a struggle. They actually get more stressed out before they even have a chance to see a change. They feel like things aren't getting done, and they're leaving in the middle of something important. But usually, after the third day, the logic of setting a time restriction starts to gel. They begin to understand that they've actually been doing the same amount of work but in a longer stretch of time.

Even if they had been diligently working every minute of those long days, the new schedule forces them to think about how they can work more efficiently in the time allotted. They have to figure out how to make a reduced schedule work—either by automating or outsourcing—in order to optimize their time. Interestingly, I've seen a 100 percent success rate with this exercise. People love it because they wind up getting more work done and, ultimately, they have more free time. It's a win-win across the board.

Time restrictions can also be applied on a microscale, for example, when it comes to how long a person is willing to spend on a certain activity. Meetings are a great example. Inevitably, most meetings can be reduced to fifteen minutes. The whole concept of meetings feels antiquated in general, especially given the technological capabilities available today. We're not in the *Madmen* days of advertising where all of the department heads need to get together once a week to update the boss on their happenings. Meetings should not be the place to inform anybody of anything. If there is important information to convey, communicate via a method such as Slack. That way, the person can send the information during the time that he or she is most productive and the person reading the information can do so at his or her most productive time, which is one of the main benefits of asynchronous communication. Meetings should be reserved for making a collaborative decision or conducting a team brainstorm.

FIGHT THE CLUTTER

Most of the time, the real issue is there are simply too many options. As a society, we almost have too much freedom and too many options. Freedom can lead too quickly to idleness and "idle hands are the devil's workshop." When people have too much freedom, or too much time to complete a project, they'll use it. This theory is the basis of Parkinson's Law, which states "work expands so as to fill the time available for its completion." If you have a task to complete, and you give yourself an hour to complete it, you'll take the full hour. Alternatively, if you give yourself twenty minutes to complete the task, you will likely get it done in that reduced amount of time. If you wait until the last minute, the task will only take a minute to complete. Similarly, a wardrobe will expand to fill all of the available space. Essentially, we take up the space we are given, which begins as a problem of having too much freedom.

There are plenty of people who self-identify as deadline driven. The fact of the matter is that everyone functions better with constraints. Open-ended projects have a way of never getting finished, so this reinforces the notion that we must set limits on ourselves. Time limitation is working effectively for my clients who now need to leave the office at 5:00 p.m., no matter what. But it works well in other realms too.

Setting limits can apply to physical spaces as well. If you're a pack rat and have rooms filled with clutter, tell yourself you're permitted one box of clutter per room and that's it! I've become aggressive regarding how many physical books I keep on my shelves, because even the bookcases can start to feel overwhelming. I receive so many free books at conferences and by doing podcasts, that if I'm not careful, I will literally be drowning in books. I give a lot of them away or send them to people as gifts, but I try to keep my own personal stash down to about ten to fifteen. Those remaining books don't necessarily represent the cream of the crop, but they are the ones I refer to or show people most often, and I've gotten rid of what I don't need or use.

If you need some guidance on the joys and how-tos of decluttering, check out Marie Kondo's book, *The Life-Changing Magic of Tidying Up: The Japanese Art of Decluttering and Organizing.* There's a reason it was number one on the *New York Times* best-seller list. She says to look at everything you own as a relationship and ask yourself the following questions: Does this relationship bring me joy? Does it bring me anguish? Or does it bring me nothing? Does that jacket I bought five years ago bring me the same sense of excitement it once did? If not, then it's time to get rid of it.

This process of setting limitations can almost become a game, and you need to figure out how to work within your restrictions. In a sense, you're working backward to the end goal or desired result. I'll give you an example of how this backward thinking can help you get to the desired result faster. A recent business venture of mine is a virtual assistant company, which I'll tell you about in detail a little later. One of my clients wanted help recording something on TV. His appointed assistant gave him some pointers on how to set a recording on the TV, but it was too much for him to figure out, and he was getting frustrated.

I happened to notice this exchange and suggested that he simply ask the assistant to record the show for him. We wound up taking it a step further and skipped the entire recording step. The assistant was able to locate what the client was looking for on YouTube and sent him the link.

We need to retrain ourselves to think about the end goal first. What do you actually want to accomplish? The client's predicament was a symptom of having too much freedom. If you don't have the constraints in place that force you to figure out solutions, you'll just end up being lazy about it. It's human nature.

THE DIGITAL DIET

Self-imposed time constraints can have a powerful impact on your day and, by extension, your life! I realize not everyone has the flexibility to dictate what time they will leave the office and 5:00 p.m. simply may not be feasible for employees in a corporate environment. However, people in a rigid corporate environment can impose other restrictions on their workflow and their day. For example, try limiting the amount of time you spend on e-mail to an hour and see what happens. Humans have an abundance of ingenuity when it comes to innovation and invention, but they somehow lack the ability to apply the same level of ingenuity to themselves.

Technology, convenient though it is, can also be one of the greatest time sucks in a day. Most people can relate to the stress of trying to keep up with the latest communications tools, apps, upgrades, and downloads. The very vehicle designed to make our lives easier and faster has morphed into a gigantic distraction. How can we reharness technology to make it work for us? By setting limits on the ways in which we use it and focus on *making it work for* us.

I've definitely had to put myself on a digital diet and streamline some of the applications I use to cut down on the distraction. Clutter on your phone or laptop can be just as distracting and damaging as clutter in your living room or office. You can apply the same principles you would use to manage your physical space to your digital space.

At one point, I was determined to have only Chrome, Dropbox, and Skype on my computer. The cloud allows for less clutter on the computer, and it's a safer alternative to the built-in hard drive, not to mention accessible from anywhere. What changes can you make to free up space in your digital world and simplify your life?

I'm just as rigorous about cutting the clutter on my phone as I am on my laptop. My iPhone has more storage than my laptop, because I literally run my business from my phone. Nevertheless, I am constantly deleting or condensing the apps on my phone to make sure that I'm actually using the items in my space. I only have two folders of apps: one for the essentials and one for everything else. If the app is not absolutely critical to my life, I'll delete it immediately.

One reason I am able to stay light with the apps is because most of those companies have fantastic web versions, so the app is not entirely necessary. I have about a dozen bookmarks on my Safari app for companies I use most frequently. For example, Uber on Safari is just as efficient and fast as it is through the app. It depends, of course, on how often you use the service, but I generally only use Uber once a month, so I don't need to clutter up my screen with the app.

MINIMUM OR MAXIMUM?

The limits you set for yourself can be very arbitrary, even artificially restrictive in some cases. For example, if you stay at the office until 8:00 p.m. every night and then start leaving at 7:00 p.m., you're not really stretching yourself. Deciding to leave at 5:00 p.m. imposes a greater restriction on your time, which in turn will force new behaviors. The famous entrepreneurship coach, Dan Sullivan, is a proponent of this concept. He says that "double" thinking is actually very bad for the brain. For example, you will challenge your brain if you are trying to figure out how to double your annual revenue or double your market share. It's almost too obvious. A healthy challenge for the brain would be to figure out how to grow by ten times as opposed to two times. Thinking about growing your annual revenue by ten times forces you to stretch and reach into places you've never gone before.

Within the context of setting limits for yourself are also the varying concepts of minimum versus maximum limits. Minimum limits are actually more challenging than maximum limits. It's easier to be restrictive than it is to be expansive. For example, it's much easier to say, "I have to turn the TV off by ten o'clock at night" (maximum limitation) than it is to say, "I will read ten pages of nonfiction every night" (minimum limitation).

Minimum limitations are particularly effective when it comes to exercise. The limitation essentially allows you to create a habit. Once you create a habit and couple it with another, your rate of potential success skyrockets. When it comes to working out, start by finding something that you love to do and set a small goal. You're never going to be successful if you come up with a running plan, but dislike the act of running. Set yourself up for success and do something that you actually enjoy. Next, find another activity that you love (watching Netflix, listening to podcasts) and tell yourself you cannot indulge until you have accomplished the first goal. Better yet, if you can combine the two, you're setting yourself up to win. Tell yourself that you can only listen to podcasts while you're on the treadmill. In that scenario, you've set up a restriction to help you succeed.

Time is an easy limitation to set because everyone is strapped for it and wants more of it. This is the main reason why people come to me in the first place. They don't feel like they have enough time to do the things they want to do. I help show them that they actually have a lot more time than they think they do; they're just not using it efficiently. By taking time away from them, they are forced to find a solution. And it works every time.

Money is another area that is fairly easy to control through limitation. I can look at someone's finances and say, "Listen, you're not allowed to spend more than $100 on dining out in a week. You can break that $100 up however you want, but after you spend it, you're cut off." This is an effective strategy to get people to eat at home more often, save money, and eat healthier. Setting limitations in one area of your life tends to have a compounding effect in other areas as well.

Of course, I advocate that people need to find a balance between challenging themselves and being realistic in terms of their lifestyle. There needs to be a clear path with small action steps to achieve the goal. The solution doesn't necessarily need to be obvious, but it has to be able to be broken down into bite-size pieces.

For example, it's too overwhelming to tell someone to lose 10 pounds a month. Maybe that is the overall goal, but it will feel significantly more manageable if we say, "You need to lose between 1 and 2 pounds a week." Present yourself with the intermittent steps that are necessary to achieve the big picture. Think about a runner who sets a baby goal of making it to the next stop sign on the street. The likelihood of him getting there is significantly higher simply because he has a goal. Not only are the microgoals infinitely more achievable, but they also give us motivation to push forward. Small hinges swing big doors and, to that end, I believe in setting microgoals in everything we do.

In my own life, some might say I have taken the concept of setting limits to an extreme. This is 100 percent by choice, and the way it manifests shifts ever so slightly depending on what's going on at home with my kids. Currently, I have a two-day workweek, which shakes out to be Mondays and Wednesdays from 9:30 a.m. to 2:30 p.m. I work my ass off during those hours. The schedule has forced me to give up a lot of things, which ultimately has been a good thing. I don't spend much time wandering around trying to figure out what needs to be done. I know exactly what needs to get done and how much time I have to do it.

Even though I teach and train people to set restrictions on themselves to have more control, *I still struggle sometimes.* However, whenever I do set limits, I always reap the benefits. I travel a lot for speaking engagements, which is a lucrative pursuit, but one that obviously takes me away from my family. I miss them desperately when I'm traveling, so I've recently limited my travel to just twice a month.

Setting limits forces people to strip away the mental and physical clutter, including all of the activities or things that are not absolutely essential. Thus new opportunities for joy, relaxation, or learning can move into the space created in the absence of unnecessary activities or thoughts. Think of a box, which is finite. In order to add something new, you need to take something out to make room. You have to identify the most important things to keep in the box. This same concept applies to time and space, both physical and digital, and is the essence of optimizing.

Three Steps to Less

1. Impose limitations to find lost time, space, money, and joy.

2. Create deadlines and meet them. Set microgoals.

3. Think of the end first and work backward.

PART II

...

AUTOMATE

AUTOMATION IS THE SECOND STAGE IN THE JOUR-
ney toward less. Think about what goals you would like to
achieve. What does the overall outcome look like? Then
take it a step further. Think about the things that you
are doing everyday and how they can be done for you.
Psychologically, automating can also be called the art of
letting go. After you have tracked your behaviors and given
some thought to optimizing your time, you are ready to
let some of those activities go.

Essentially, automating means examining all of the bite-
size tasks leftover after optimizing and determining what
software and/or processes can be used to get them done
without human interaction. Whether or not you decide
to use technology to automate, it's important to consider
what triggers a specific action.

For example, if you are a Twitter user, look at when you
go onto the app and what you are doing when you get
there. Personally, I look to see if anyone has mentioned
my name. If someone has mentioned me, what do I do?
Do I respond to the person? Do I save the comment? When
you look at actions on this level, you start to identify a
chain of steps and the order of the process. From there,
you can begin to make that process more efficient. What
about the process can be automated?

In the nontech realm, there are hundreds of ways that you can automate activities around the house to save time. For example, we have one of those simple human garbage cans at our house. It requires special fitted bags, which can be a real pain in the neck if you're not prepared. But when you get down to the second to last bag, a little red tab pops up that tells you it's time to reorder. That red tab is a trigger that leads to an action, and it's those types of triggers that we need more of in our day-to-day lives.

Five

THE DECISION MATRIX

• • •

THE THREE DS

The decision matrix refers to three critical action steps: delete, defer, or deal. This concept ties into the idea of limiting our options, which we covered thoroughly in Chapter 4. When faced with a task, you need to break it down and ask yourself if this is something that you can (or should) pass off to someone else, deal with it and move on, or say no to right now.

When people think about saying no to something, the tendency is to fear they are missing an opportunity. For example, when I am invited to a speaking opportunity and think about saying no, I worry about what the consequences will be. How might the decision to say no hinder me or prevent me from moving forward in my career? Is it the loss of income that causes me worry, or am I concerned about my limited exposure, or a loss of connections? Asking yourself, "Can I say no to this?" is a very subtle shift from, "Will I or won't I do this activity?" When you put the question in the context of *can you say no to it*, you are allowing yourself more control over your decision. If someone were going to offer me a million dollars for the speaking opportunity, then likely, *no*, I couldn't say no to it.

The next question is can you do this activity right now? Is it something I can do later or defer to someone else? For example, you realize you need to make a doctor's appointment at nine o'clock at night. Maybe you personally cannot do that right now, but you can ask your virtual assistant to take care of it for you. If you ask the assistant now, then it's taken off your plate and deferred to him or her. There is a tremendous amount of freedom in delegating the task to someone else, because you get it out of your own head and off your own dreaded and ineffectual to-do list.

If you're extraordinarily efficient and have systems in place to deal with the decision matrix, you can accomplish tasks in minutes. For example, while I'm on my way from one room to another at home, I can check e-mail on my phone and decide whether to delete, defer, or deal with the new messages. If your options are limited to those three choices, it's very easy to assess and decide. The "deal with" category includes delegating, so even if you decide you need to get an assistant or someone else involved, you've still made a decision (deal by delegation), and you're still making progress.

E-mail seems to be one of the most common sources of stress in people's lives, and it is practically universal. I've worked with stay-at-home moms and high-level CEOs, all who feel weighed down by the e-mail burden, which is really the burden of inefficient communication. Luckily, it's one of the simplest issues to resolve. The decision matrix makes e-mail straightforward and even easy to get through. You can handle e-mail in one of three ways: delete it, deal with it, or defer it. Once you have this strategy ingrained in your thinking, try to find other areas in your life where you can apply it.

The ultimate goal of employing the decision matrix is to achieve ABD: always be done. We're always trying to be done in one way or another, but in order to get there, you first have to understand what being done actually means to you. Being done is entirely subjective, and I've found that people on the whole need to change their perspective about what it looks like. Setting microgoals is an important tool when trying to ABD. On a subconscious level, every time we complete a task, no matter how small it is, we feel a sense of accomplishment, which inspires us to move ahead to the next task.

Virtual systems have a time shifting ability that is critical when it comes to automating tasks and ABD. Think about this scenario. You're lying in bed at the end of the day getting ready to go to sleep. Your mind is churning through the day's events and what you need to do tomorrow. You remember suddenly that you need to make an appointment to see the dentist. Of course, the dentist's office is not open at 10:00 p.m. when the thought occurs to you to make the appointment. So what do you do in this situation? Do you write a reminder to yourself on a post-it note beside your bed? Do you send yourself an e-mail reminder? Do you make a note on your calendar? Better yet, why not send the appointment request to a virtual assistant? That person is obviously not going to make the appointment immediately, for the same reasons that you can't do it yourself, but nevertheless, you are done. You're done worrying about it, thinking about it, and even doing it. All you have to do is show up when the virtual assistant tells you to (and don't worry, the assistant will typically have access to your calendar). There is nothing more that you can or should do and therefore, it is off your plate.

The minute something comes off your plate, or a micro-goal is accomplished, you're done! This doesn't mean you need to rush through things, but you are shifting the focus from the endless to-do list. Instead, you break up your day into a series of small goals. If you are able to write two hundred, or complete five phone calls, or send ten e-mails, you are making small steps—each of which should feel satisfying—as opposed to one sluggish step in a sea of endless steps. There are infinite opportunities to accomplish the feeling of "done" along the way.

I was working with a client one time who literally had twenty-seven tasks on his *Saturday* to-do list. We were talking about how problematic this was during one of our weekly calls. He was disappointed that he wasn't able to get everything done. Ultimately, he abandoned the list midstream because he felt guilty that he wasn't spending time with his family.

We decided to go through every single item on his list and apply the decision matrix to each of the tasks. Unsurprisingly, he could immediately (and easily) deal with over 75 percent of the things on the list by delegating. The remaining 25 percent of the tasks were absurdly large. In fact, the most absurd thing of all is to make a list with twenty-seven items on it that you want to accomplish over the weekend (but I digress). One of my favorite things on the list was to learn how to play the song "Patience" by Guns and Roses on the guitar. I got a good laugh out of the irony of that one. Not only because of the title of the song, but the task in and of itself is self-defeating. Very few people can sit down and just learn a new song on the guitar in a day. He could, however, learn two to three main chords and go from there.

I think about task delegation and automating as similar to the game, Brick Breaker. You want to have as little "touch" as absolutely needed on a project. Once you've made the decision to automate the task or outsource it, you're done. You don't want to hold on to it just for the sake of holding on, and you don't want to spend any more time on it than necessary. Once you receive the task, then immediately get rid of it, like the ball in Brick Breaker. When you become an expert in the decision matrix, your little ball (or all of the tasks on your to-do list) will fly up the side of your wall (or list) and smash all of the bricks (or tasks) at the top until you are free to bounce all over the room (or your life) unhindered by all of those things that kept you walled up for so long.

VISUALIZATION

My son's speech therapist introduced me to a new visualization exercise recently. I've found it to be incredibly useful with my clients and in my own life, not to mention it's been wonderful for my son as well. At the beginning of the session, they sit down and map out what they are going to work on that day. Then the therapist asks my son to draw what they are going to do, usually in three boxes, each one representing a different activity. The exercise helps my son to organize, psychologically, what they're focusing on in that session. It also gives him a sense of control; he is helping to make the schedule, and there is clarity around what's ahead within the session.

I tried this exercise with a few of my high-level CEO clients and found the visualization element combined with the sense of self-control to be powerful. At the same time, it can also be humbling. The exercise strips out all of the fluff and the noise that surrounds an activity. Even if you're an excellent artist, there is a limit to the level of detail you can put into a drawing. If you have a career-changing call with the CEO of IBM scheduled one morning, how can you convey all of that pressure within a drawing? You can't! The best you will likely be able to do is draw a picture of a telephone, which mentally helps to simplify the task at hand. The simplicity of the act of drawing psychologically distances you, in a good way, from the pressure of the moment and the actual work product.

The truth behind the activity is you are making a phone

call. It doesn't matter if you are talking to the president of IBM, a disgruntled customer, or a potential client. The action and the skill is the same regardless of who is on the receiving end. If you sit down and map out your morning in a series of three simple sketches, in the order in which you will do them, you will experience a definitive mental shift. The whole point of the exercise is that you cannot overthink it. No matter how high level you are, or how many important things you have to do in a day, when you boil it down to a stick figure on a piece of paper, it helps to bring you back to reality.

The visualization exercise is perfect for the average over-achiever. You may do hundreds of things in a single day, but if you're able to focus on the top three activities you need to and draw them out, I guarantee you will get them done! This tactic does not work with technology. You need an old-fashioned pen and a piece a paper. But it does work across languages and cultures, and it's a practice that dates back to prehistoric cave drawings. Since we are always trying to be done, the beauty here is it decreases the amount of decisions you need to make to get there. Would you rather make seven decisions or one?

> *"Civilization advances by extending the*
> *number of important operations which we*
> *can perform without thinking of them."* *
>
> ALBERT NORTH WHITEHEAD

We waste energy if we take too long to make decisions. The three pillars of the decision matrix—delete, deal with, or defer—prevents the mental fatigue that occurs when we try to switch back and forth endlessly between tasks. We have the capacity to make automated decisions, as outlined by classical psychologists Skinner and Pavlov, through mental conditioning.

The first thing you need to do is put your ego aside. A lot of the people I work with are under the (false) assumption that they are the only ones who are able to do a certain activity. This is unhealthy thinking, and besides, it's not true. If you are of the opinion that you are the only person capable of doing something, you likely haven't examined the process of doing that specific process.

Regardless of your position or your stature, other people or other things can do the vast majority of the things you do on a daily basis. The sooner you can accept this reality,

* www.brainyquote.com/quotes/authors/a/alfred_north_whitehead.html

the better off you'll be mentally and the more time you'll have. Research shows that we should off-load and delegate approximately 70 percent of the activities we perform year over year.

In addition to the types who think they are the only ones capable of doing certain things, there are also the types who tell themselves, "This will only take a minute." Almost nothing only takes a minute, and if it does, you are probably taking yourself away from something else that you are in the middle of. There is an opportunity cost in that line of thinking. Research shows it actually takes about twenty-three minutes to get back into a flow state.

International best-selling author, highly regarded psychologist, and winner of the Nobel Prize in Economics, Daniel Kahneman, explains the two systems that drive the way we think in his incredible book, *Thinking Fast and Slow*. System one is our autopilot mode—the state in which we go through most experiences in life. The second system is the deeper, more analytical mode, which requires more energy. Our brains are constantly trying to push us to use the autopilot system, where things are automatic. This includes activities such as taking a shower, brushing your teeth, driving to work, or checking social media. Driving and talking on the phone (always with a hands-free device) are also automatic behaviors. When our brains drift toward autopilot, we lose touch with the steps in the process and stop thinking about how we could do it better or faster.

We want to take full advantage of the automatic system to put the overwhelming majority of our daily tasks on autopilot. I use Kahneman's theory on my clients who think they are the only ones who can do something. When they are adamant that no one else could possibly do what they do, I push back and ask them to explain to me exactly what it is they do. Together, we dig into the processes and the steps behind an activity. Once we look at the activity from an analytical perspective, they are able to understand they are not, in fact, the only person capable of completing those steps.

The autopilot mode affects our emotions as well. We react habitually to certain experiences, which determines how we behave in relationships, in business, and at home with our families. For example, heartbreak causes us to be more cautious and guarded the next time we enter into a relationship; the wall will go up in an automatic response to protect ourselves from future pain. We have the option to change that behavior or response. It's a matter of asking yourself if you are willing to trust or if you want to approach new people with an edge of doubt. This forms the basis of CBT or cognitive behavioral therapy, which tells us that we are not our thoughts and that our reactions to certain events are within our control. This, of course, requires a healthy dose of self-awareness.

TRAINED BEHAVIORS

Technology can affect our consciousness as well. If you're someone who likes to keep your phone on vibrate, you've probably experienced phantom vibration, which is a real psychological syndrome when people have the *perception* that their phone is vibrating, when it is not. It's actually a very common phenomenon. We have programmed ourselves to always be on the alert for a vibration and are therefore highly attuned to anticipating it, just like Pavlov and his rats!

The same sort of automatic response occurs if your boss comes by and drops a pile of paperwork on your desk. Your automatic reaction will likely be a feeling of dread or stress. You can train this feeling away. Think about a Navy SEAL who doesn't blink an eye or get flustered when bullets are whizzing around his head. The SEAL is trained to stay singularly focused on the task at hand and to not be distracted by anything, even bullets. Any practitioner of martial arts can understand a SEAL's trained behavior. Krav Maga, for example, is an Israeli self-defense system that combines techniques from several other martial arts and teaches automatic responses to aggressive behavior from others. The responses are designed to finish a confrontation quickly and efficiently with attacks aimed at the most vulnerable parts of the body.

In the same way that you can train yourself to react in a life-threatening situation, you can also train yourself to behave a certain way when you are at work. Scientific studies have proven that if someone is smiling when they speak on the phone, the positivity transfers and the other person will mirror the action. In general, humans tend to mirror behaviors anyway, so it makes sense that the behavior would be replicated on the telephone. If you can train yourself to smile every time you pick up the phone, you will have more productive calls. This practice aligns directly with how someone handles their e-mail inbox too. If you know that you can handle every e-mail in one of three ways—delete, deal, or defer—you won't even have to think about it, and you'll save buckets of time.

The decision matrix allows for automatic behaviors to become ingrained, thereby dramatically increasing productivity, while also eliminating decision fatigue. It also establishes a formula that you can apply across all areas of your life and trains you to quickly assess your three options and choose one of them. Utilizing the decision matrix is the first step in understanding how to automate.

The closer you can get to being "done" with a task, the freer you will ultimately be.

Three Steps to Less

1. Implement the three Ds: delete, deal (including delegating), or defer to all tasks.

2. Strive for ABD: always be done.

3. Put your ego aside and recognize that sometimes the hurdle is you.

Six

SET IT AND FORGET IT

· · ·

ACTION TRIGGERS

Once something has become a recurring task in life, the very nature of it should be an automatic signal to start looking for ways to get rid of it! Ron Popeil, the famous inventor and marketer, is known for the phrase, "Set it and forget it." He was talking about a rotisserie chicken, but the phrase taps into the heart of automation. It's a concept that originally resonated with housewives in the 1960s, but the implications are more applicable than ever in today's crazed world. The notion of using a slow cooker to prepare meals is still a popular one with anyone who wants to get a jump start on the week's meals. Batch cooking can be a real time saver.

There are tons of areas of our lives that Popeil's brilliant advertising phrase has impacted. Simply by "setting it," you've triggered an action of some sort. This comes into play naturally throughout all areas of your life. Think about the thermostat; you set it to a certain temperature for different periods of the day, and that's it, the temperature is regulated. If you put the lever up on the mailbox, the postal carrier knows to retrieve outgoing mail on the delivery route. My wife and I have two dogs, and they eat different kinds of food. We order their food in bulk, and their cans are different colors. I switch them so when I pull one out that is toward the end of the supply, it's coded so I know it's time to order more. I use Amazon Prime for a lot of basics around the house. I have a standing order for AA batteries and Brita filters. Every six months or so I receive a shipment of those items and when they arrive, I know it's time to refresh the batteries in the smoke detectors and change the filter on the Brita. Over time, the triggers become automated behaviors. The thing to note here is that you can always look for ways of removing yourself just one more step from a process. In the aforementioned example, I could have set a reminder in my calendar every six months to place an order, but removing myself one more step means the order is placed for me, and I don't have to do anything at all.

Technology can take you to the moon and back when it comes to setting up automatic tasks. My favorite website and tool for managing it all is IFTTT.com, which stands for "if this then that." It's a free site and can be used from anywhere in the world. It performs very simple automated tasks among various sites. For example, if I update my profile picture on Twitter, IFTTT.com will also update my photo on Facebook and Instagram. The accounts are all linked, so I don't have to perform the same task three or more times. It may seem like a miniscule task, but if you are trying to manage multiple platforms, this level of automation can make a world of difference. Plus, the task may only take sixty seconds, but if you are doing it twelve to twenty times a day, the time saved adds up quickly. In addition you are setting yourself up to avoid errors, which has its own value multiplier.

Once you start to chain daily tasks together and automate them through a site like IFTTT.com, you can create extremely complicated processes that in some cases might add up to an entire person's position. The hope is that the person can then focus on performing more relevant, meaningful, and rewarding tasks.

The best example I have about how this has worked for me in my own life is how I have automated my podcast production process. I went from spending fifteen hours an episode to an hour per episode (the hour that truly only I could do, and the only part of the process I actually enjoy doing)! The process was a huge time suck because I am not skilled in graphic design, audio editing, or script-writing. Once I realized I could farm those tasks out to people who were talented in those areas, the entire process became streamlined and actually enjoyable. Today, the podcast production is completely automated and requires almost no effort on my behalf, and yet I still reap tremendous benefits from the output, as do my clients and wider Internet audience.

The technology and systems behind my podcast production process are as simple as they come. The way it works is I save the master audio file to Dropbox, which triggers IFTT. From there, IFTTT sends the file to a graphic designer, to a company called Rev for transcription, and to an audio engineer for editing. They all deposit their files back into Dropbox, which again triggers IFTTT to automatically combine everything and post the final file to my blog, my website, and my social media platforms. There are checks and balances for quality built into the process to ensure that the outcome is in line with my brand. Basically, I record an episode and three to four days later I see the end result on my own blog for the first time.

All of the steps within the process are extremely low cost yet highly reputable and repeatable. I am producing one podcast a week, but I could easily scale up to a daily production with the current system I am using. I don't have to worry about anyone calling in sick or forgetting a step. It is a virtually error-proof process that runs itself. I have about 120 separate processes set up in IFTTT to run on a daily basis. To be clear, that means 120 things I don't have to do or think about.

The most important benefit of setting up systems is that it gets the activity off my mind. Yes, it saves time and yes, I no longer have to actually do the task, but freeing up brain space is the highest value add from my perspective. Setting up "set it and forget it" processes allows for peace of mind and the knowledge that things have been handled in a timely manner. This works especially well with the ever-nagging, e-mail inbox. Automated e-mail processes, such as filtering into pre-named buckets, remove the doubt and uncertainty around whether you responded to an inquiry or not. You simply know it's been dealt with and can think about other, more important things.

Setting up systems and processes, particularly through a site like IFTTT, is incredibly simple and user intuitive. You don't need to be a tech geek to reap the benefits of establishing automated processes. They offer hundreds of services to streamline usage of some of the most common apps and websites that you're likely already using multiple times a day. Simply select the apps that you use most frequently, and the site will show you how to set up common triggers and actions.

One of my favorite "recipes" is the voice mail to transcription text. It personifies the external brain concept perfectly. Whenever you have a thought that you don't want to forget, you can call IFTTT and leave a voice message with your idea. A few minutes later, you'll receive a text message (or whatever form of communication you specify) with your thought transcribed and organized. You can even have an automation set up to send the text to Evernote with a tag, so it is transferred immediately to your data collection area. Voilà, thought saved for a rainy day.

Once something becomes a recurring task in your life, that should be an automatic signal for you to start looking for a way to get rid of it. Managing your postal mail is an excellent example. The US Post Office recently announced a new service in which you can have all of your mail scanned and e-mailed to you in advance or in lieu of receiving it in your mailbox. They already scan all of the mail anyway, so implementing this new service is not too much of a stretch. The service is only available in a few zip codes, but it's coming to a city near you very soon!

There are so many things that we do in a day that we don't stop to think about. We just do them a certain way because that's how we've always done them, for example, paying bills online. We tend to think it's fast and efficient to use online banking to pay the bills. The truth is that we can easily automate every monthly bill. Sometimes, there's even a cost incentive to set up automatic recurring payments. But how many of us actually have set up the automatic billing? There are hundreds of things like this in our lives every day. We just never stop to look at *why* we do things the way we do them. The reason we don't scratch the surface is because it takes effort, a commodity most of us are pretty short on already. The truth is it's a transferable skill.

Zapier is another automation service, and it's slightly more sophisticated than IFTTT. It allows you to set up extremely complex systems. My partner and I are actually running our virtual assistant business (more on that in Chapter 9) largely through Zapier. It's the glue of the company and handles everything from hiring and training new staff, onboarding new clients, billing, sales and marketing, and time tracking. All of those critical functions are automated through Zapier.

IDoneThis is yet another service that helps keep track of your tasks. It sends you an e-mail at the end of each day, detailing what you accomplished. Essentially, it creates a journal that summarizes what you've done. In the same vein is Call Frank, which you can program to call you at the end of the day. It gives you sixty seconds to share the day's highlights, records your feedback, and tracks the information. If you have a problem waking up to an alarm, you can use WakerUpper, which is a robotic wake-up call. It's a great backup service for when you cannot afford to oversleep for that early breakfast meeting or 6:00 a.m. flight.

Automating, in a big sense, is about loosening the reins so that you can go faster. By relinquishing a little bit of the control people like to cling to, you actually experience greater freedom. I've noticed the hardest thing for people to let go of is e-mail. It's almost like the thirteenth step of the twelve recovery steps. Delegating e-mail is not necessary for everyone. About 50 percent of the people I work with are on that level. For the person who has a huge volume of e-mail, it can become a necessity.

We are very fortunate to live in a time when automation has become so easy. It's practically negligent to ignore the technologies that can make our lives so much simpler and more enjoyable. The possibility exists to greatly reduce and eventually eliminate the amount of time between a trigger and an action. If you don't need to be involved in either, why would you be? The choice is yours! It comes down to the question, do you want it to be good, or do you want it to be yours?

Three Steps to Less

1. Identify and create a plan to off-load 70 percent of the tasks you perform daily.

2. Set up systems through IFTT.com to manage automated tasks.

3. Relinquish control and experience freedom.

Seven

ATTACHING A NEW HABIT TO AN EXISTING ONE

• • •

WHENEVER WE CAN CREATE A HABIT OUT OF AN activity, it becomes automatic. Creating a habit—in and of itself—is not automatic, but with a little practice, habit forming becomes a mind-set and an overreaching goal. When an activity becomes a habit, it becomes second nature. It's no longer something that we think about doing; we just do it, and therefore we conserve mental energy in the execution of said activity. As a result, we do not tax our brains by hopping back and forth between activities. In this way, we can use the autopilot mode of our brains to our advantage.

Multitasking, as we've discussed, does not exist, and it certainly does not maximize our human potential the way some employers would like to think it does. However, it is possible to "fake multitask" by combining a high-focus task with a low-focus task, for example, watching the news while brushing your teeth. It depends, of course, on how your brain is wired, but I am able to go through e-mails while listening to a podcast. Neither of those activities are particularly high focus or high energy for me. E-mail management is something that has become almost automatic thanks to the three Ds, and because the resources required are so low, I'm able to get through my inbox while also doing something additionally productive.

MULTIPLE PLATFORM REPURPOSING

I am highly attracted to activities or processes that I can repurpose and retool. Brendon Burchard, a famous performance and personal development trainer, has mastered the art of repurposing content. Every week, he records a thirty-minute motivational YouTube video, which is automatically turned into a podcast. The podcast is transcribed and repurposed into blog posts, and from there, the content is broken down even further into Instagram posts for his followers. Burchard's thirty minutes of effort becomes multiple outlets with which he can reach his audience and provide value.

One of the reasons I am so inspired by Burchard's practice is because it's easy and seamless to implement and takes advantage of something he is already doing. It requires almost zero effort beyond setting up the initial automated steps. He has taken an activity that he is already in the habit of doing and maximized the impact by repurposing the content across multiple platforms. Everybody has the ability to maximize at least one of their activities in a similar manner, thereby making a larger impact with the least amount of effort.

I truly believe that everyone on the planet has some sort of unique genius to offer. I think most people are unable to share this unique genius with the world because they don't have enough time or there is some other restriction that is preventing them from sharing it. Even if you're not a frequent blogger or podcaster, the chances that you are already doing something in your daily life that is a source of valuable content is extraordinarily high.

If everyone were able to share their unique genius, the world would be an infinitely better place. I recognize this idea might sound naïve, but I am committed to my belief. There's got to be someone, somewhere who happens to be amazing at making miniature figurines out of walnut shells. By the same token, there are likely at least a hand-ful of other people, somewhere in the world, who would really like to learn how to make miniature figurines out of walnut shells. If you start looking at the things that you do in your spare time, or even the activities that you do to relax, chances are strong that there is an audience for your knowledge or expertise somewhere out there.

I was working with a young mother recently. Every night she makes a beautiful homemade dinner for her family, and it's something that she takes great pride in doing. I suggested, in the spirit of Ree Drummond, the Pioneer Woman, that she start taking pictures of the meals as she prepares them and post the pictures to Instagram. Then she can have a virtual assistant automatically post the photos to Pinterest, write a blog for her about the recipe, and provide a source of inspiration and information for other moms out there who are looking for ideas about what to cook for their families every night. My young mother client has been doing this for a few months now, and she absolutely loves it. She's gained some followers and has had a healthy interaction with other people "out there" who are in the same boat she is.

I started following the Pioneer Woman's blog early on, because I love her sense of humor and her pictures. She quickly rose to one of the Food Network's gold-star chefs, she's made millions on her blog, and she is a number-one *New York Times* best seller. It all started when she was homeschooling her kids in Oklahoma and writing about it. Her first food blog was "How to Cook a Steak." It was accompanied by about twenty photos and as she says, "a ridiculous amount of detail" about the cooking method. She's won numerous blogging distinctions and is even in talks to make a Hollywood film based on one of her books. Talk about capitalizing on your unique genius!

Not everyone is going to achieve the same fame and notoriety as Ree Drummond, but it is within all of us to share our specific knowledge with a wider audience. Salespeople, for example, typically record all of their sales calls. They could easily have those calls transcribed and summarized into a how-to e-book on sales. The cost to do something like that is extremely low, but the potential broader impact is significant. We all have activities like this that we do every day, almost without thinking, that we could maximize into something larger.

On the one hand, there are the types of people who think that everything they do is amazing. And then there are the types of people who think that no one would care about what they are doing. They think it's mundane or boring, such as cooking dinner for their families. The truth is plenty of people are stymied about what to cook for dinner. The mere thought of it is overwhelming and dreadful. Even if the photos my mom client puts up on

Instagram and Pinterest, or the e-book the salesperson creates from his calls impact only one person, the minimal effort and cost will have been well worth it.

HABIT FORMING

By definition, a habit is a routine behavior that one regularly repeats, often without thinking. What are your habits and how can you effectively attach additional habits to the one firmly fixed in place? In the case of Brendon Burchard, he is in the habit of making a thirty-minute video every week. The subsequent actions (podcasts, blog posts, Instagram posts) are a by-product of the original habit, but he doesn't have to actually do anything beyond the initial setup. They happen as a result of an existing habit.

If you are trying to establish a habit, such as running every morning, there are specific physical steps you can take to increase the odds of the habit forming. For example, if you put your running shoes right next to your bed and set the alarm for the same time each morning, you are setting yourself up for the habit to stick by removing obstacles to your success. When you wake up in the morning, you're a few steps closer to getting out the door and going for a run.

The morning commute is a time period ripe for establishing productive habits. For example, I know a lot of people who have made it a habit to call their assistants on their way to the office to go over the day's agenda. This step saves time upon arrival at the office, because you can launch immediately into the day's activities without stopping to check in with your assistant. You can set reminders to help yourself along in this endeavor by placing your phone next to your car keys.

Additionally, you can use technology to help you remember an activity you are trying to make into a habit. There are apps and programs that can send you an automated message at a specific time each day that says, "Call your assistant." Alternatively, you can easily delegate by asking your assistant to call you every morning at 7:55 a.m. It might even be as simple as a post-it note stuck to the dashboard. The point is there are any number of ways to go about reminding yourself to start an activity that will eventually become a habit.

The issue, from my perspective, is that so few people actually utilize their downtime to create habits, let alone attach one to another. Sometimes, the highest level of productivity someone is able to achieve is reading the newspaper or browsing through e-mails on the train. People tend to label certain activities as productive but wind up setting unrealistic goals for themselves. Also, very few people actually use their commute time to get a jump start on the day.

In order to better utilize precious time, set aside a minute (or twenty) to record your thoughts, either through an audio device or even write in a journal. It doesn't matter what it is; it could simply be that day's stream of consciousness. Allow your ideas to flow, free form, and after about a week's time, you will have established a habit. The important thing is to start. Create an open pathway in your brain to get new ideas churning and old ideas downloaded, in the spirit of utilizing the external brain.

If you're one of those people who cannot remember to call your mom, set up reminders for yourself on hassleme. co.uk. The reminders are incredibly simple to set up and you'll stay out of the dog pound. You can even set the reminders for random blocks of time so that calls to mom or flowers for your wife appear to be spontaneous, as opposed to rigidly fixed every Tuesday or Friday. The random feature can be applicable for many activities, and it feels more genuine and makes the activity less of a chore if you do it every twelve days. Plus, you may not actually buy your wife flowers every week or so, but the reminder prompts you to think about it.

BATCHING

Batching is essentially grouping similar tasks together so that you can avoid multitasking and focus on similar tasks all at once, even if it's only for a brief amount of time. Fifteen-minute increments are perfectly functional. There are two separate benefits associated with batching tasks. The first and most obvious one is to avoid the brain drain that occurs when switching from task to task, which is a common side effect of trying to multitask. There are certain tasks that have a sporadic nature, which lend themselves nicely to combining in that they take considerably less effort.

Mail is a perfect example. Most people receive their most important information via e-mail these days. The majority of things that arrive through the US Post Office are junk: flyers, coupons, circulars, catalogs. I process all of my mail on Fridays, because I know if there is something really pressing that I need to know about, I'll hear about it via e-mail or text. Whatever is waiting for me in the mailbox is not urgent and can wait.

If, for some reason, there is a bill that has not yet been digitized, I will have to do something about it. Usually I take a picture of it, upload it to Evernote, send it to my accountant, and then go online to pay it. Those are fixed steps involved in receiving a bill. It's not a time-consuming endeavor, but it does add up. Therefore, if I receive two or four bills a week, I definitely batch them together and pay them all at once. This goes back to why I only check my mailbox once a week. If there is anything in there that I need to deal with, I can take care of all of it at once on Fridays.

Another efficient batch activity is cooking. My older son has gotten to an age where he really enjoys helping out in the kitchen. On Sundays, we cook huge batches of sauce or soup for the week. We make lunch sandwiches for school and dinners for the days ahead. This is a massive time saver in that no one has to worry about making dinner during the week after a long day. Plus, we have a lot of fun deciding what to cook, doing the shopping, and preparing meals together on the weekend. The efficiency and immediate benefits of batch cooking can be a real game changer when you're trying to get the kids out the door for school or don't feel like cooking after a tough day.

I'm always looking for ways to save time, and attaching habits to existing habits has been one of the most effective ways to maximize activities. I often schedule phone calls when I know I will be walking my twins to sleep in their stroller. Their naptime is the same every day, so I know that I have a golden hour from 10:00 a.m. to 11:00 a.m. each day when I can focus on a conversation, get the boys to sleep, and squeeze in some exercise too. It's a triple-header. I usually walk about three miles; both of my hands are on the carriage, and I am completely in the zone. It's a very utilitarian endeavor.

I almost never schedule phone calls for longer than fifteen minutes. I view calls the same way I view meetings. I typically schedule four calls of fifteen minutes each during my daily walk around the neighborhood. Walking the twins is a low-focus task. They're just lying there, getting some fresh air, and drifting off to sleep; we're not engaging. Talking on the phone though is a high-focus task. So in this case, I am batching activities, but I am also attaching a habit (scheduled phone calls) to an existing habit (walking the boys to sleep around the neighborhood).

I have actually become better about utilizing the conversations that occur during that window to their maximum capacity. Contrarily, if I schedule a call at 9:15 a.m., I have to stop what I am doing on the computer and switch gears entirely to a concentrated conversation. It's a disjointed process and neither activity is getting my full attention. Consequently, I almost never schedule phone calls first thing in the morning because that's my time to be on the computer with my headphones on, jamming out high-focus work during my peak time.

Think of batching as an economy of scale. When you are doing a handful of similar tasks at the same time, you are maximizing your efficiency in that particular zone. For example, if you were trying to make dinner and catch up with your mom on the phone at the same time, either something is going to burn, or your mom will feel like you're not paying attention to her.

The practice of batching goes back to the Pomodoro Technique we talked about in Chapter 2. The Pomodoro Technique is based on the idea that our brains work better in sprints than they do in marathons. The technique suggests that we work in timed, twenty-five-minute intervals, with five-minute breaks in between for maximum mental output. This practice works beautifully with task batching. Set the timer for twenty-five minutes and during that period, focus exclusively on e-mail, or phone calls, or writing, or paying bills. The twenty-five-minute periods of productivity force you to generalize and stay on task with the specific activity, as opposed to the end product.

We can apply the Pomodoro Technique to activities that some might ordinarily consider unproductive or distracting. Social media is a great example. If you want to get caught up with Facebook or Instagram, instead of feeling guilty about it, give yourself a window. It's far more productive to focus on social media for twenty-five minutes at a time than it is to check it every five or ten minutes. Just batch it! You can even treat your social media time as a reward. If you're able to complete two full twenty-five-minute cycles of focused work time, then allow yourself another twenty-five minutes of social media.

Rewards can be efficient too! It's not efficient, however, to be constantly switching back and forth between tasks and distractions.

You can play around with the ratios of work to rest, but the idea is to structure a focused sprint, followed by a brief rest.

We can apply the same technique to sleep. The scientific community agrees that one of the major functions of sleep is converting short-term memories to long-term memories, which is also tied to learning. You've heard the old wives' tale that studying before bed actually helps you to retain information longer. Science has now proven that the tale is correct. Sleep helps us to process memories (and information) properly. One of the biggest symptoms of sleep deprivation is memory loss. Without sufficient sleep, we have a hard time concentrating and remembering key information.

Edinburgh Research Explorer found that just nine minutes of rest after learning new information helps you to retain it longer. By rest they mean no stimuli whatsoever, just let your mind shut down and wander. The pause in brain activity helps to convert the information or memory into storage, where you can easily access it at a later time.

The study was conducted in one instance with people who have amnesia. They were broken into two study groups and each presented with a list of thirty words. The group that rested for nine minutes after reviewing the words was able to recall 80 percent of the words. The group that was not able to rest didn't recall any of the words. This is a truly staggering finding in that it suggests, even among amnesiacs, what people really need is the opportunity to slow down and rest so they can process new information.

The fact is the activities that people consider to be unproductive or distracting are actually activities that allow our brains to pause and reset. We need a shift in perspective to better understand the value of distraction. It's not that the activity is necessarily distracting; the problem is we are going about being distracted inefficiently. To that end, social media, or even just staring into space, are highly valuable activities. Batching them or scheduling Pomodoro time periods can harvest the inherent value of those activities. When you eliminate sporadic behaviors and tasks and bundle the identical tasks together, ultimately you are one step closer to working (and resting) efficiently.

The practice of attaching habits to other habits is highly useful in that it triggers certain actions automatically. When you connect certain activities to ones that are already ingrained, you are creating a smoother flow of actions for yourself and dramatically increasing productivity and output.

Three Steps to Less

1. Maximize your unique genius by repurposing ideas or activities into useful content.

2. Establish productive habits and eliminate time-consuming or useless habits.

3. Get in the zone by batching similar tasks together.

PART III

. . .

OUTSOURCE

OUTSOURCING MEANS REFERRING ANYTHING THAT cannot be automated to a generalist or a specialist. Essentially, it is tapping into the lost art of delegation. Our generation has a tendency to think that delegating is simply telling someone else to do something, thereby just pushing the task further down the line and not necessarily making anyone's life more efficient.

The truth is that delegation is the very heart of leadership. It's when you can effectively communicate to someone what needs to be done. Through clear communication, you are empowering the person to take ownership of the task to the extent that they can overcome hurdles or obstacles without having to come back and check in with you. This action frees you up to perform activities that are better suited to your skill set, rather than manage the person you have entrusted with a task. In an ideal world, everyone gets to focus on the tasks they perform best and most efficiently. I consider that scenario to be the perfect economic model.

Eight

THE VIRTUAL ASSISTANT

HOW IT WORKS

The simple definition of a virtual assistant is an assistant who is not in the room with you. Because of the advances in technology, anyone can do almost anything remotely. There is no longer a need to have someone physically sitting next to you, or just outside of your office, as tradition would have it.

Within the virtual assistant world, you still have the option for a dedicated assistant or you can go the route of an on-demand assistant. There are pros and cons to both. A dedicated assistant is just as it sounds. You have one person assigned to you specifically. That person gets to know you and your preferences. You can train him or her in the specific things you like: direct morning flights, aisle seats, Enterprise versus Hertz, and that sort of thing.

One negative of a dedicated assistant is that he or she is usually more expensive than an on-demand assistant. Also, if that person gets sick or can't make it to work for whatever reason, unless you have backup systems in place, there will be a bottleneck. You're in the same boat you'd be in if Judy, the secretary you've had for fifteen years, comes down with the flu.

An on-demand assistant is on the other end of the virtual assistant spectrum. There can be thousands of assistants in the pool. Without much preamble, you upload your task and any one of them can pick it up and get to work on it. Usually these are low-focus tasks that don't require a lot of explanation, such as making reservations or setting appointments.

There are several advantages to on-demand virtual assistants. Attractively, on-demand assistants are almost always less expensive than dedicated assistants. You can have support 24-7 because there's always someone in the assistant pool ready to get to work. The pool will be made up of people from a wide variety of skill sets and backgrounds, which comes with its own set of benefits. You can issue a larger volume of tasks and there will never be a bottleneck.

Strangely enough, the lack of a personal relationship makes it easier to pass off tasks that one might otherwise consider menial. For example, the first book I wrote was about green building materials because that's the field I was in at the time. I worked on it for close to three years and there were over 180 companies referenced in the book. Just as I was finishing the final draft, the publisher said I needed to go in an update all of the contact information for every single company mentioned for the reference section. I thought, "Okay, this is awful, but it has to be done."

There was no way I had the time to call 180 companies, and they all really did need to be called. We couldn't search through the yellow pages or check online. I realized I needed help, and it was the first time I hired a virtual assistant. This is exactly the kind of task that anyone (outside of a hopeless jerk) would feel weird about asking his long-time assistant to help with. It's a terrible, time-consuming, thankless, menial task, but it had to be done. On the other hand, it's very easy to give a task like this to a virtual assistant. They're happy to do it. Whether you are personally aware of it or not, the virtual assistant company would likely have six different people working on that one assignment and it would be complete in twelve hours.

Alternatively, you could issue ten different assignments at once and ten different people would jump on board to get it done. That's the way it works!

The downside, however, is that you typically cannot hire a virtual assistant to handle time-sensitive or overly complicated tasks. (A task is generally defined as an activity that can be completed in approximately twenty minutes.) It's unlikely that you will share passwords or financial information with a virtual assistant, so the relationship has its own set of limitations.

LESS DOING

Delegating to a virtual assistant is one of the most productive activities anyone can undertake. In fact, a friend of mine and I started a virtual assistant company called Less Doing Virtual Assistants. We employ the highest trained, most capable project managers and virtual assistants in the business. The idea was born from a mass e-mail sent out by the top US-based virtual assistant company, Zirtual. With zero warning, they sent an e-mail to their 2500 customers and 400 assistants that said, "Thank you for being a part of the family. Due to financial difficulties, we will be closing our doors."

The e-mail caused an implosion. If anything constitutes

breaking news in my world, this was it. I had been referring clients to Zirtual since they started and overnight, they destroyed the trust of their customers and staff. My clients and friends were texting and e-mailing me wondering what they were going to do. Then, to make matters worse, the very next day they sent a second e-mail saying, "We're okay. We figured everything out last night, and we're back in business." Needless to say, they easily lost 90 percent of their clients due to their erroneous maneuver and never recovered from the damage.

That same night my friend Nick and I were having dinner. He said, "Well, Ari, why don't you step in to claim the market share from Zirtual?" I didn't want to go through the headaches of managing all of those people and a brand new business, but the opportunity was undeniable, and he agreed to help. In thirty-six hours, we were up and running. We built the whole company using completely free tools such as IFTTT, Zapier, Trello, and Slack. I sent out a tweet saying we were hiring. We hired three or four ace virtual assistants, and we were scalable and profitable from day one. We've grown exponentially since then. Not to mention, it's the ultimate lean start-up. We started without any outside funding, zero overhead, and almost no expenses. This led to the creation of an entirely new division of Less Doing, called Less Doing BPO or Business Process Optimization. We took all of the best practices we learned, and continue to learn, and help businesses of all sizes optimize, automate, and outsource their processes.

Less Doing Virtual Assistants moved in to fill a space that Zirtual vacated, but we also took it a step further. Most virtual assistant companies are populated with people who can perform tasks and/or do a little research. They can make a dinner reservation or doctor's appointment, and they can find and send the perfect gift, but our assistants can also do project management. We can literally do anything that a business owner needs us to do, at very low cost to them and extremely reliably. We've produced podcasts and sold cars; we've even set up an entirely new business for a client in Pakistan. We've never had to say "no" to a client request, which is a significant differentiator in the virtual assistant space.

We have trained all of our assistants in my specific productivity methods—the same ones I am sharing with you here in this book. We continually work on training our assistants to be faster and better than anyone else in the field. This experiment has also allowed me to uncover a different side of my coaching clients, because I get to see how they interact with the assistants. I can very clearly see what types of projects they are delegating and how well they are implementing some of my productivity strategies.

Less Doing is essentially a hybrid of dedicated and on-demand virtual assistants. We have a core team of about sixteen assistants, all of whom are highly trained and can work with pretty much anyone who comes along. Our clients tend to work with the same assistant for several projects in a row; they naturally gravitate toward one another. We also have people who can jump in on any twenty-minute task that comes along, so we have a nice mixture of capabilities.

The perfect economic model, as envisioned through the effective use of outsourcing, unfortunately does not exist (yet). The virtual assistants at my company are highly trained and therefore they wind up even further outsourcing some of the tasks that come across their desks. They are savvy enough to know they don't need to be bogged down with menial tasks that other people, programs, or systems that are less trained or skilled could perform.

IDENTIFY THE ESSENTIAL

As we well know, some people are of the mind-set that they're the only ones capable of performing certain tasks. They erroneously believe their unique perspective must be stamped on virtually every task and activity within their department or company. Although grandiose, this "do-everything" mind-set is incredibly limiting.

There is simply no way to grow or move forward if you are the cog in the machine that runs everything. If you want to take a break, or a vacation, what happens to the output? If you break down, the machine breaks down. Plus, if you are the one person doing everything, you are going to quickly become overwhelmed, if not shut down, and at the very least, slow down. It doesn't make sense from any vantage point to put yourself in a position where you are 100 percent essential.

There needs to be a balance between the absolutely necessary and the off-loading of nonessential tasks to achieve optimal workflow, peak output, and productivity. There is no shortage of resources out there to assist you in off-loading up to 70 percent of your daily tasks so that you can be freed up to grow as a person. I like to use the analogy of a snake shedding its skin or a snail getting a new shell. Similarly, we must let go of the old to make way for the new.

If you are able to identify tasks and activities that you can off-load and outsource, it means that those tasks and activities are not essential to you. There is a better way to go about getting them done, and most of the time it's by someone or something else. Often times, this comes down to mind-set. Most of my clients, particularly when I first meet them, are not in the mind-set to outsource, let alone automate. Like almost everything else in life, it takes some practice and a little bit of discipline to get there.

I'll give you an example of one of my virtual assistant clients. One, of many things, that he does is help authors reach number-one, best-seller status on Amazon. He had a Filipino assistant who logged onto Amazon every hour and took a picture of the book's ranking. The client wanted to know if this was a service we would be able to provide. Yes, of course, we could easily have an assistant perform the same task as his guy in the Philippines. However, more effectively, we could build a program for $120 that would check the book status and take a photo every minute, or even every thirty seconds for as many books as he wanted. His mind was blown. The problem was his mind-set was fixed in a limited space, and he couldn't see the larger potential.

Limited thinking is a problem I see all the time in most of the companies and organizations that I work with. People simply don't tend to look for another, better way of doing things. They say to themselves, "This is how I've always done it and it works just fine." The saddest part in this line of thinking is they truly believe the tasks and activities they are performing are essential and there is no other way to go about getting them done. There are other ways and other options! Hiring a virtual assistant is one of the most economical and efficient ways to off-load tasks.

The cost of hiring virtual assistants is still relatively low. Five years ago, all of the virtual assistants were based out of India, but the market there became flooded and the quality of work went downhill. Even if someone spoke perfect English, there was still a high margin for error if even just one word was incorrect because it threw people off.

The virtual assistant business isn't exclusive to administrative work. I use a company called Design Pickle, and they do unlimited graphic design work for a fixed fee. They help with blog post images, photo correction, website updates, and anything design related that might pop up. The options are truly unlimited in terms of finding reliable, affordable, outsourced help across industries.

Many people have a built-in resistance to the idea of hiring virtual assistants. I'm not sure if it's generational or psychological, or what the hang up is, but if you are someone who is resistant to this idea, ask yourself why.

Overall, people are okay with asking for help, but they have a hard time assuming a leadership role, even when it comes to their own lives. In business school, there was a class called Management 100, which focused on the topics of leadership and communication. Early on, the instructor gave us two-dimensional structures and asked us to organize them in a way that represented the correct organization of a team. Everyone had a different interpretation and structured the figures differently, but for the most part, the figures wound up in a pyramid or a circle. The gist of the exercise was to illuminate that there is a place for leadership, but to be a good leader does not mean pushing everyone else down. You can raise yourself up, but it doesn't have to be at the expense of others.

Some people are of the mind-set that in order to be useful, they need to take ownership over every little thing. This behavior can sometimes feel almost defensive, and it has to do with the fact that as a society we perceive busyness as a good thing. The fact of the matter is that it's not cool to be busy! It's not cool when you don't see your family because you're working too much. There's no nobility in that predicament.

Delegation is a muscle that you need to exercise like any other. You must use it to create pathways in your mind and create channels to get things done. Not only is it important to be more efficient, but it's also a vital part of the decision matrix we discussed in Chapter 5. People have a hard enough time saying no as it is, so if delegating is not an option you allow yourself, you're going to feel even more hard pressed to say yes and get in over your head.

When working virtually with anyone—an assistant, a designer, a team member, or a boss—clear communication is of the utmost importance. Even with Skype and all of the technology we have available for remote access, there is little margin for error or nuance, which forces you to become more efficient with your words. A nice side effect of clear communication is it helps to speed up the process by which we get work done. The person receives the assignment, the directions are clear, and away they go.

We've discovered there are certain types of people who actually perform much better when they are away from others, working autonomously. Yes, this scenario is contrary to most corporate cultures and the all-pervasive team mentality. However, there are a lot of task-centered people out there who love to work on one thing at a time, do it very well, and then be done. When we can match people like this with people who are overwhelmed, magical things happen: we remove bottlenecks, we complete tasks quickly, and everyone functions within optimal work zones.

The virtual assistant business started to take off when individuals realized that they needed to outsource some help. When people see their "to-do" list magically shrink, the benefits of delegating start to catch on. It's the difference between putting something on your to-do list and feeling stressed out every time you see it and giving it to someone else who can get started on it right away. By the time you've thought about the task again, it's finished, and you can move on to the next thing. Visualize your to-do list and an army of people working on it to get things done. The satisfaction of that visual should trigger an action—ideally delegating!

The virtual assistant industry has seen a lot of changes in just a few short years. I see a huge potential for outsourcing in large companies and businesses with over one hundred employees. When you can make individuals as efficient as humanly possible, the companies they work for will also reap the benefits. Individual efficiency is at the very heart of what I strive to help people achieve.

The range of services that virtual assistants provide is astonishing. There is literally someone for every aspect of your life that will save you time, money, and aggravation. For example, if I wanted to have this book translated into Spanish, which eventually I do, I can put the entire project in the hands of a virtual assistant. This saves me the time and hassle of finding a translator, interviewing book designers, finding a layout person, and everything else that goes into a translation. Instead of me personally handling five to ten steps, one person can take care of it all far faster than I would ever be able to do it. Does your driveway need snowplowing? Are you searching for a specific class for your child? Do you need someone to take over the payment of your monthly bills? The list is virtually endless.

On the business side, virtual assistant capabilities are equally diverse. We have an event scheduled in the next few months, so we have a virtual assistant working on a website for us. Because it's a workshop, we need a landing page, graphics, sales copy, and a promotional video. The VA is handling all of that for us. We've used VAs for everything from e-mail marketing campaigns, social media, content repurposing, travel and event planning, and holiday or promotional gift mailings. Some of these tasks are high touch in that they require knowing the specifics of our business or personal preferences, but some of them fall under the category of standard administrative tasks.

A few of the companies we work with have latched on to the idea of virtual assistants in a big way and provide them for every single one of their employees. When a company recognizes the value and utilizes VAs for personal tasks, in addition to business functions, we know they really get it. They have accepted or adopted an almost Google-like stance, recognizing that if people aren't worried about picking up their dry cleaning at noon, they can focus more intently while they are at work.

Once you've created a process that is replicable, it becomes intrinsically scalable, which means the output potential is exponential. Hiring a virtual assistant (or ten) is the first step to developing an outsourcing mind-set and guarantees to immediately free up large pockets of precious time.

Three Steps to Less

1. Hire a virtual assistant (or ten).

2. Understand the difference between necessary and nonessential.

3. Always look for ways to remove yourself from the process and exercise the delegation muscle.

Nine

OUTSOURCING YOUR OUTSOURCING

. . .

TYING IT ALL TOGETHER

The process I lay out to combat the experience of being overwhelmed and dealing with chronic stress is to optimize, automate, and outsource. Although these three practices do follow a nearly linear pathway, they can (and should) be combined and used in harmony for various tasks. One should explore the possibilities that open up when you go essentially up and down the ladder of the three strategies.

Experimentation and implementation leads "automatically" to scalability. There is almost no limit to what can be outsourced. The process and the plan will look different for everyone, but when you loop a virtual assistant into the mix, the sky's the limit.

Even when you're working with human capital, there is an automated component to it. For example, the process that I use with my podcasts has automated steps along the way and only involves human capital when absolutely necessary. We have stripped out all of the back and forth that typically occurs when a boss asks an employee to do something. The tasks are stacked in a way that one specific action triggers the subsequent actions and there is zero time-consuming discussion about it. It's like clockwork, and I don't even have to think about it.

The whole podcast operation runs almost like a racecar with a pit crew. The car spins around and around the track at top speed and peak performance. Every now and then, the driver has to stop so that a pit crew can rush in and do the maintenance for the next batch of laps around the track. It's like a condensed Pomodoro Technique—maximum efficiency in fixed time bursts.

Productivity will reach an entire new level when you begin to outsource your outsourcing procedures. There are two ways of going about this. The first is when you are triggered to automatically bring in people (virtual assistants) as needed. And the second is when the additional people outsource the outsourcing. Today's world is rich in technology options and those options are only increasing by the day. The volume of services and the number of ways in which we can reach other people is too much to keep up with. Most highly trained virtual assistants can't even stay abreast of the development. There are actually outsourcing experts these days who are completely in tune with the latest and greatest developments throughout the industry. Any virtual assistant worth his or her salt will have a few outsourcing experts in their contacts, because every good generalist needs a few specialists.

The fact of the matter is people simply don't know what they don't know. If you're someone who has no clue about the technology available to make your life easier, the necessity for you to find yourself a "project manager" for life is even higher than the average person. My father, for example, has no idea that there is a service (Postmates) that will deliver meals from any restaurant in Manhattan straight to his door in under thirty minutes. He doesn't know there are bike messengers (UberRUSH) who will make pickups and deliveries throughout the five boroughs. He doesn't know there are laundry services (Boomerang NYC) that come and pick up your laundry and bring it back—clean and folded—the very same day. He doesn't know about Magic or GoButler or any of the other incredible conveniences that have popped up in recent months and years to simplify and streamline your daily life.

In the on-demand and sharing economy in which we live, most people will need someone to help guide them through the forest of options and synthesize the information to find the right provider and the right pathways. It might sound ironic or contrary, but the truth is an outsourcing expert is the way to go if you're a newbie to the outsourcing mind-set. For example, my dad would benefit tremendously from someone who understands his specific needs and can help him to outsource his outsourcing! He needs an expert who can deal with the logistics of optimizing and automating and then, finally, outsourcing certain tasks and activities.

Even for those in the know, the new user interface is "no user interface." A few years ago, cutting-edge companies focused solely on the website, then it was the app, and now it's neither of those. Magic is one of my favorite recent inventions. It's a dedicated text service that takes instruction and makes delivery on virtually any (legal) request you can think of such as: deliver a dozen long-stem white roses to my wife tomorrow, or I need a helicopter from the downtown Manhattan heliport to New Canaan in an hour, or book a four-star hotel in downtown Dallas for the weekend. Magically, as the name implies, your request is fulfilled. It's different than other similar services because you communicate only via text; there is no app and no website, so it's almost a level above the rest.

"Set it and forget it" is the new normal. This dynamic allows for tremendous peace of mind from just knowing that the tasks you need to take care of are already cued up and ready to be dealt with. On some level, once you adopt this mind-set, thinking about optimizing, automating, and outsourcing becomes second nature. I know it has for me. Back in the day, I never even considered how a project or task could fit into any of the three approaches. Now I won't start on a new venture unless all three of the criteria are met.

Most people get themselves into a situation and then backtrack toward optimization. But to be truly efficient with your time, think about the potential for optimization, automation, and outsourcing from day one. That way, you are setup to grow straight out of the gate. Maximum productivity comes down to an issue of volume. Don't start doing a podcast a week until you have thought through the logistics of how you can output seven in a week. In some ways, this is simply another way of saying, "Think big!" Don't limit your own potential by thinking in bite-size pieces of only the work that you personally can handle.

Beyond hiring a virtual assistant, there is a wide range of outsourcing services, big and small, for any task under the sun. For those who are looking for assistance beyond task management, there are also a number of project-based specialists. We've covered a few areas where project-based specialists are beneficial, but if you are facing any of the following, outsource!

- Research projects
- Social media management
- Ghostwriting
- Financial modeling
- Travel planning
- Event planning
- Graphic design
- Website creation

Certainly, you can bring in professional organizers to handle anything that might fall under the category of "life management." This includes all of the errand-type activities I mentioned earlier when I was talking about my father. Typically, I am pretty anti-errand, because I know there are an abundance of low-cost services that can save mountains of time and untold aggravation, such as laundry delivery, meal and grocery delivery, messenger services, shopping, driving, child care, and home repair.

You name it!

You can easily customize an outsourcing plan tailored to your unique needs. For example, if you are trying to eat healthier but don't have the time to cook or shop, there are a number of incredible nutrition and personal chef plans available.

Essentially, automation is the future. Humans will always be fallible, there's just no way around it. They get sick; they have personal problems, bad days, family emergencies, and other unexpected human realities that pop up to slow production. Automation makes things cheaper, more error resistant, scalable, transferable, and repeatable. An automated process is never going to get tired, or call in with the flu, or complain, or quit unexpectedly. On the flip side, your human employees will also be happier because they don't have to do that tiresome work anymore. You are basically reallocating resources so that you can utilize your people and your processes to the best of their abilities. Automation is the first and most important step in the productivity improvement process.

When you have reached the point of mastering optimization, automation, and outsourcing, you are able to get back to basics, which allows you to enjoy the simple everyday tasks that you may once have eschewed. The phenomenon reminds me of the scene in Bruce Almighty, when Morgan Freeman (as God) is mopping the floor with Jim Carrey's help, and he says, "No matter how filthy something gets, you can always clean it right back up again." I think about that line when I'm doing the dishes at the end of the day and find myself actually enjoying the simplicity of the task.

Three Steps to Less

1. Remove yourself from the equation entirely.

2. Seek expert outsourcing guidance.

3. Optimize, automate, and outsource. Discover what it means to be human. Take it a step further to avoid outsourcing by automating completely

CONCLUSION

* * *

THE THREE-TIERED PROCESS OF OPTIMIZING, AUTO-
mating, and outsourcing is designed specifically to help
people feel more human. Far from transforming people
into thoughtless robots, the idea is to use the processes and
systems afforded to us by technology to reclaim precious
time and to pursue the things in life that you love, ideally
with the people you love. The process will free you up to
focus on the things that you want to do, instead of grinding
away endlessly on tasks that someone or something else
can easily perform.

Scientifically, humans are creatures of leisure. No matter
what time period or circumstances we live in, we need to
have time for relaxation, reflection, humor, and overall
downtime. We are not created to be "on" and functioning

all the time, despite the go-go-go nature of our culture. The more we can maximize our downtime both in quantity and quality, the better we'll be able to perform when we do need to be "on." Even our children don't have enough time to just play and be kids. As we get older, we get further and further away from our natural state of wonder and curiosity.

I am very fortunate to pursue a career that allows me a measure of fun and joy. To me, finding ways to work less and do more through, optimization, automation, and outsourcing is fun! My goal is to teach others to connect the dots and find the enjoyment in found free time, too. The end result of what I consider to be playful manifests itself as real change in my own and other people's lives.

There is hard scientific data that supports the benefits of playfulness and rest. Research has proven that certain activities, such as washing the dishes and folding laundry, are a gateway to mindfulness meditation because your mind is able to drift and recuperate when performing these tasks. We need to give our brains a rest from working hard so that we can enjoy and truly experience all of the other things that make us human: culture, love, community, service, and learning. Without those rewards, we face burnout, joylessness, and a feeling of desperation. In those circumstances, we become completely ineffective.

We need to be putting so much more energy into making ourselves happy, relaxed, educated, and improved so that we can put 20 percent of white-hot-fire intensity into the work that we do. This approach is far more impactful than taking a lukewarm, mediocre stance on everything we do in our lives.

Most of the people that I consult with are simply trying to live normal and rewarding lives. At the end of the day, people basically want the same things: peace of mind, time to relax, less worry, better results from their efforts, appreciation, and less stress. But unfortunately, most people are completely overwhelmed, and they don't know which end is up. There are also a good handful of people I work with who are looking for the 1 percent edge. They are highly functioning, high-net-worth individuals, but they want to perform better and still have more time to enjoy the fruits of their labor.

The solution for both types of people is the same. It does require a little bit of soul searching, however, which is not always an easy endeavor. People need to think about what is fulfilling for them, which can mean different things at different times in life. Fulfillment also touches people on multiple levels: emotional, physical, spiritual, cultural, financial, and more. There was a time in my own life when I was sick that I was 90 percent focused on physical fulfillment. Over time and with the growth of my family, my focus has shifted to emotional fulfillment.

Just recently, I was running around the city with my twin boys. There was a problem with our car, and I needed to drop it off for repairs on the Upper West Side. While on my way uptown, my friend, also named Ari, who is in medical school in Kansas City, texted me about how badly he was missing NYC bagels (There really is nothing in the whole world like them, especially not in Kansas City!). I decided I would kill several birds with one stone, which is the heart of optimization. I dropped the car off, I put the boys in their stroller, we walked to the park and played for a little while, and then we went to the bagel shop across town. We started walking back downtown because it was time to drop the twins off at school. On the way downtown, I ordered Shyp to come and get the bagels and send them to Ari. Shyp is an on-demand shipping service, and the way it works is you take a photo of the item you would like to send and about twenty minutes later, someone shows up (wherever you specify), they make a box, and ship it wherever you need it to go. I dropped the boys off at school and took the subway back uptown to get the car from the shop.

I suppose I could have handled the mornings' tasks in any number of different ways. I could have had TaskRabbit come and get my car and take it to the shop uptown. I could have used PostMates to get the bagels for my friend Ari and sent them through Shyp. I could have used Task-Rabbit to collect my car again when it was fixed. But then what would I have been doing all morning? There's always work to be done, but instead I walked six miles, spent time with my kids, personally selected bagels for my friend, and I even recorded a video and created content. I accomplished far more meaningful results than I would have if I stayed at home.

There's an element of pure enjoyment built into the full-circle nature of task delegation. In some ways, productivity is born from a lack of productivity. The chaos forces us to create systems if we want to be more productive, efficient, and effective.

What changes are you going to be able to make in your life and, hopefully, in the lives of the people around you? What will that change look like for you and for your wider community? When you can tap into your inner motivation and discover what drives you, you'll be a lot closer to taking the steps necessary to get there.

If you're like so many others, you may not have the first clue of how to answer the aforementioned questions. Happily, there is an effective method to get to the heart of any problem called The Five Whys. You identify a problem and then drill down into The Five Whys behind it. I'll give you are very simplistic example to illustrate how this works.

Problem: My tea was cold.

Why #1
The kettle didn't heat the water.

Why #2
There was no power.

Why #3
The fuse in the plug was blown.

Why #4
An incorrect fuse was being used.

Why #5
The required fuse was not specified.

Solution: We need to get the right fuse to use in the future.

* * *

This method, centered in factual responses, is reliably effective to find solutions to problems. The practice works just as well when looking at bigger problems beyond the tea being cold.

The very good news is it is possible to make significant change in your life without a huge amount of effort. All of the strategies and practices we've discussed in this book are right there for the taking! By simply being more conscientious about your time and your choices, you can free up precious time to enjoy doing the things you want to do. Ironically, in becoming more efficient, you will find beauty and value in retaining certain inefficiencies. You will also, undoubtedly discover where there is a benefit in doing things for yourself. Ultimately, through the process of optimizing, automating, and outsourcing, you will make your life better. Through education comes improvement and with improvement comes satisfaction. Less doing = more living!

ACKNOWLEDGMENTS

My wife, Anna, who never lets me get away with a sub-par performance, no matter what.

My sons, Benjamin, Lucas, and Sebastien; you give me reasons to constantly improve.

My co-founder Nick, the perfect partner.

ABOUT THE AUTHOR

. . .

ARI MEISEL is an author, speaker, coach and the creator of Less Doing, More Living, a set of practices and principles designed to help the overwhelmed become more effective.

These practices were born out of Ari's battle with Crohn's disease. As his illness progressed, he began to optimize, automate, and outsource *everything* in his life so that he could completely focus on healing his body.

Inspired to help entrepreneurs and companies Ari now teaches them how to offload the majority of their activities so they can grow, prosper and spend more time doing the things that *truly* matter most.

CPSIA information can be obtained
at www.ICGtesting.com
Printed in the USA
FSOW02n0845170817
37710FS